THE FRUGAL PILOT

How to Fly on a Budget

by Dan Ramsey, *The Frugal Pilot*™

FrugalPilot.com

MULLIGAN PRESS

SMART CONSUMER GUIDES

THE FRUGAL PILOT
How to Fly on a Budget

by Dan Ramsey

Published by Mulligan Press.

First Edition

Print Book ISBN: 978-0-9706131-0-3

Electronic Book ISBN: 978-0-9706131-1-0

Portions of this book were previously published under rights from the author issued to *General Aviation News*.

Disclaimer: This book is not intended as flight instruction. Refer to the U.S. Federal Aviation Administration or your country's aviation regulator for flight and aircraft rules and regulations. Fly safe!

Visit The Frugal Pilot website at FrugalPilot.com.

Email the author at Dan@FrugalPilot.com.

Contents

Introduction

Flying can be expensive!

Flight schools typically charge about $10,000 for instruction required to become a Private Pilot. The newer Sport Pilot certificate is less expensive, at about $6,000, but still not cheap. You can fly an Ultralight aircraft that doesn't require a pilot certificate, but you still should get training, typically about $2,000, to be a safe pilot.

Then there's the cost of going flying. The typical pilot spends more than $10,000 a year on aviation including aircraft loans, insurance, hangar rental, fuel, and required annual maintenance. To keep "current" on skills and experience, many general aviation pilots come up with excuses to go flying, such as flying to a distant airport restaurant for what's referred to as a "hundred-dollar hamburger."

Aircraft aren't cheap, either. A new four-seat airplane costs $200,000 or more. A two-seat Light Sport Aircraft (LSA) typically is more than $100,000. Even used aircraft that are older than their pilots can cost $25,000 or more.

What's the solution for bringing down the cost of going up?

Thirty years ago, I wrote a best-selling book titled **Budget Flying** to help new and experienced pilots discover the many safe options they have for flying on a budget. Today, I am a still frugal (smart use of resources) pilot with practical knowledge of how you can earn a pilot license and enjoy flying on a budget.

How big of a budget? One pilot traded his professional skills to a flight school in exchange for lessons. Another is using legitimate aircraft deductions in business to reduce his tax obligations. Many join partnerships or flying clubs to reduce flying costs. Others are thinking like smart consumers to save money on every aviation purchase, from aircraft to fuel to headsets. None of these smart aviators can fly for free – but they can reduce the costs of flying and get more enjoyment from each dollar spent and mile flown. And so can you! You can be a Frugal Pilot!

What makes an airplane fly? Money!

Who gets the most flying for their money? A Frugal Pilot!

--Dan Ramsey, the Frugal Pilot™

FrugalPilot.com

P.S. - Not yet a pilot? The final chapter offers a BONUS summarizing what you need to become a pilot – on a budget. Enjoy!

10 Tips for Frugal Pilots

Flying is fun! But it can be expensive: mandated maintenance, rising fuel costs, airport expenses, and fly-in restaurants. They all add up. Fortunately, there are many proven ways of bringing down the costs of going up. You can fly more and spend less by discovering how to be a frugal – not cheap – pilot. Here are my ten favorite tips.

Tip 1: Remember why you fly.

Life quickly becomes complex without any help from us. What starts out as a dream of flight soon becomes aircraft payments, hangar leases, insurance payments, avionic upgrades and unexpected maintenance bills. And those costs are exponential to the aircraft we select. Owning a simple Cessna 150 is much less expensive to fly than is a Cessna 182RG. He gets places faster, but I can go the same places – and a few he can't. Frugal pilots consider why they fly – recreation, business, short hops, cross-countries, family vacations, solo cloud-inspections – and select an airplane that is most cost-efficient for their primary flying goals. They then can periodically rent an aircraft for those once-a-year flights that stretch their horizon and their budget.

Tip 2: Keep it simple.

Kind of related to remember your flying goals is making sure your aircraft is no more complex than you really need to meet those goals. Many pilots choose IFR aircraft at additional purchase and maintenance costs when they only fly on instruments a couple of times a year, and only to stay current. If your reason for flying doesn't require an instrument aircraft, avionics and recurrent training, consider simplifying to a VFR-only plane – and saving money. And if local weather is temperate and your aircraft is aluminum, consider renting a tie-down rather than a hangar, saving yourself a few thousand dollars each year.

Tip 3: Manage your wants.

When (not *if*) I win the lottery, I have a list of cool stuff I want for my airplane – including maybe a couple more planes in my new executive hangar. Until I hit the lottery (maybe sometime after I buy a lottery ticket), I plan to stay within my needs list. Does it make my airplane safer? Will it save me money in the long run? Is it a smart purchase toward my flying goals? If it survives these questions, there's a good chance it's a "need" and will get purchased. Otherwise, it's a "want" and must await my lottery winnings.

Tip 4: Be smart about aircraft maintenance.

It seems like an airplane is always begging for maintenance. And much of it is legitimate stuff that needs to be done to be safe and avoid repairs. But some of it really isn't critical – at least not yet. Determining what is necessary maintenance and what is not can be an expensive difference. The best advice is to *learn* your airplane, not just the Pilot's Operating Handbook (POH) but the parts book and the service manual, too. Then *listen to* your airplane. You will soon be able to read its sounds to know if something doesn't sound "right" before it needs a repair. Also remember that Time Between Overhaul (TBO) is an *estimate* of the flying you'll be able to do between engine overhauls. Knowing your airplane can help you extend its life by hundreds of hours – and cut your costs by thousands of dollars.

Tip 5: Learn from your experiences.

Keeping good records on your aircraft and the flying you do can make you a frugal pilot. For example, tracking oil analysis reports over the years can tell you if you are using appropriate additives. Figuring out how and when to lean your aircraft's fuel mixture is useful information that you can track and take advantage of. Also track oil usage between oil changes to determine if something is changing in your engine that you can't see. A simple notebook with dates, meter times, actions and observations can help you get the most from every dollar you spend on your airplane.

Tip 6: Learn from smarter pilots.

No matter what you fly or where, there's someone nearby who knows more about aviation than you do. Unsolicited advice can be annoying, but finding smart pilots who can teach without lecturing is an opportunity to improve your skills – and lower your flying costs – without having to depend on just your experiences and your pocketbook. As you identify these smart and helpful pilots, cultivate their friendships and save yourself a ton of money. And consider membership in aviation clubs that fit your needs: AOPA.org, EAA.org, etc. Also help your aircraft mechanic with the annual inspection, if allowed, by removing inspection plates and the aircraft interior and learning more about your plane.

Tip 7: Shop smarter.

The Internet is amazing. With it you can read product reviews, compare prices and find the best resources for just about anything aeronautical – including the best aircraft mechanic. And by keeping written track of your aircraft (Tip 5) you also know what you'll be needing for maintenance during the next flying season or two. For example, you can buy a couple of cases of oil and a few filters in advance for both quantity discounts and free shipping. Some flight instructors offer discounts if you pre-pay for services. Shop for your plane as you shop for any high-ticket item: do your homework and shop smart.

Tip 8: Barter and trade as you can.

If your flying budget is tight, like mine is, there are many ways to cut your flying costs without spending much money. You typically can borrow once-in-a-lifetime tools from other owner-pilots. You can trade some of your professional skills for flight time, instruction, maintenance, repairs or another aviator's surplus equipment. Consider bartering or trading the next time you reach for your flying wallet.

Tip 9: Multitask flying.

Flying your own aircraft is an opportunity to travel for a variety of reasons including business, pleasure and training. As you plan your next flight, consider multitasking. Make a tax-deductible stop at a client's on the way to your family vacation. Take an extra ten minutes during your next fly-out to practice slow-flight or precision turns. Plan a mid-trip stop in your next cross-country to visit old friends. Multitask.

Tip 10: The bottom line.

A frugal pilot is not a cheap pilot. Nor is a frugal pilot unsafe. *A frugal pilot is one who makes common-sense decisions toward getting good value from every flying activity and dollar.* Fly more and spend less as a frugal pilot.

Frugal Pilots Remember Why They Fly

The first tip for frugal pilots is: *Remember why you fly*. That kind of makes sense, but it is quite easy to forget as we start thinking about all the options and opportunities we pilots have. Faster aircraft, new electronics, upgraded instrumentation, a fancier paint job – they all vie for our interest and our wallets. But do we need them? Maybe.

The problem is that *complexity increases costs exponentially*. Upgrading simple VFR (visual flight rules) instrumentation, for example, to IFR (instrument flight rules) can easily multiply costs by a factor of four or more. If it's required for safe flight, such as frequently flying out of a cloudy home airport, it's a necessity. If it's only required once or twice a year, it's really not a necessity; it's a want. Maybe it still should stay in your budget, but only after the safety and other vital needs are met.

Recent economic changes also can make you rethink your flying budget. Maybe your job was downsized, you're considering cutting back on your toys or you're planning for an imminent retirement and want to fly more. In any case, it's a good idea to review the costs of flight.

The solution to overspending is to periodically analyze why you fly and to come up with a realistic mission for your future flying. Then measure it against your flying budget. Once a year, maybe during the winter or other non-flying season, sit down with your log book and your check book to make sure they reflect your flying mission. To get your creative juices flowing, here are some typical reasons why many pilots fly:

To go somewhere. Frugal pilots often define their flying by *where* they fly, such as to specific airports, new airports, for business, for scenery, or for a great hamburger. They may also define where they go by how they go: fast or slow. Pilots often prefer one over the other.

To go nowhere. Many pilots prefer to stay near the nest, simply flying the pattern to someday achieve the ultimate goal of the perfect landing. Or they have a specific course they most enjoy flying, taking in the scenery, but typically only landing at their home airport.

To see the world from above. Many pilots fly because it literally adds a new dimension to their lives. Looking down from 2,000 feet, crab grass is invisible. Hanging in the air in familiar surroundings can be a real stress-reducer at the beginning or end of a workday or week.

To discover self. Most pilots have other titles: father, mother, husband, wife, partner, employer, employee, professional, workaholic, etc. But they all take a back seat to *pilot-in-command*. In the left seat, they are in control. And the hard work and study that brought them to this title and position gives them individual pride found in few other personal endeavors.

To share recreation. Many pilots prefer not to fly alone. The fuel costs about the same no matter whether the flight is solo or with a friend or relative or two. So why not share the ride. Maybe it's a colleague from work, a spouse, a child or grandchild, or someone who recently expressed a cesire to go flying. Flying is a gift to be shared.

To overcome fears. Not everyone feels totally comfortable in an airplane high above the ground – including many pilots. In fact, that's why some became pilots, to overcome a natural fear with the irrefutable facts of aeronautics. Once accomplished, they help others overcome similar fears. That's why they fly.

To build a professional aviation career. Many pilots fly for a living. Their private pilot or sport pilot certificate is just the first of many. It's a worthwhile goal that motivates them to select an aircraft and fund their flying, typically on a budget, to meet specific goals.

In the real world of flying, there is no single goal for any pilot. All of us have multiple goals. But one or two of these flying goals is prominent – at least for the next few years. To be a frugal pilot, first consider the primary and secondary reasons why you fly and keep them clearly in mind as you plan and purchase your flying needs for the coming year.

Plan to Keep It Simple

Every layer of complexity you add to flying – or just about anything – increases the costs of ownership, maintenance and other expenses. Instead of you owning it, it begins to own you. Soon, what started out as a fun pastime can become a stealer of time and money. Analyzing why you fly can help keep the costs on the ground.

Each of us has the same time inventory: 8,760 hours in a year. The average recreational pilot flies just 1% of that time – and thinks about flying the other 99%. On the other hand, our flying budgets range from one to many thousands of dollars a year depending on our flying goals and budgets. The average annual budget among recreational pilots is about $10,000 a year. Reviewing why you fly every few years can help you get the most from every dollar you spend and each hour you fly. That's being a frugal pilot.

My airplane had ten owners in 55 years. That's typical. The average pilot gets a new set of wings about every five years. Some may hold on to their plane for 20 or more and a few sell their aircraft after a year or two, but five is typical. So a five-year flying plan makes sense for many recreational pilots. At the end of five, some decide to hold pat and others have already moved on. At that point, some pilots simplify and others go for more complex aircraft depending, again, on recently reviewed flying goals and budgets.

The next step is to quantify your flying mission with a specific plan. How many flying hours are you realistically planning for the next five years (or whatever time frame you select)? What type of flying? Do you <u>need</u> a faster or slower aircraft than your current wings? More instruments and equipment or less? What's the least aircraft – and least expenses – you need to fulfill your flying mission? Would you be smarter to sell your airplane and rent or quit renting and buy? What about a partnership or a flying club? Are your flying goals better met with an LSA, a glider, a homebuilt, or a vintage aircraft? Just what aircraft will best match how you want to be flying into the future?

Maybe your current plane is fine for the mission, but it needs something to help you enjoy flying more. Not just stuff you want, but things you really need for your goal: upgraded avionics, more horsepower, a balanced cruise prop, tundra tires, or maybe a taildragger conversion. Here is where budgets go awry. It would be great fun to add a STOL kit, but how much will you really need it versus needing the dollars it will cost? Don't say "no." Just make sure you're getting value for what you need and can afford. Is it an extra expense or an investment?

Whatever plane you buy or equipment you add will require periodic maintenance. It may raise the cost of your annual inspection or require special STC maintenance over the next few years and these costs have to be factored into your decision. Also review FAA Part 43 that lists what preventive maintenance you, as the aircraft owner, can perform and compare it to what you feel comfortable performing. If you can save a few hundred each year on aircraft maintenance, you can spend more on your wants list.

Another aspect of simplifying your flying is reviewing where you keep your wings. You may be limited to one or two airports within your preferred driving distance. Too far away and you won't fly as often. But airports vary greatly in the costs and availability of hangars and tie-downs, even within a small area. Doing a little research may yield a more cost-effective airport for your aircraft. Some frugal pilots opt for a tie-down instead of a hangar and save enough each year to buy a quality cover – and pay for the annual inspection. Others choose a shed hangar without walls and save money. Local climate and availability will be factors in your decision.

Flying is a complex pastime – and so is choosing and funding your wings. Frugal pilots aren't cheap. They just consider all the options as well as their budget as they file a smart flight plan.

Manage Your Wants

What's the difference between a *need* and a *want*? At the grocery store, a *need* is buying milk, bread and other food staples. A *want* is getting soda, corn chips and snack cakes. In recreational aviation, a *need* is something required to meet your flying goals and your budget. A *want* is not required but desired.

For most of us recreational pilots, airplanes really aren't needs. They are wants. But one benefit to working hard through life is to be able to afford some of the things we want. However, once we own a plane, we cannot skimp on its needs.

The key to selecting which wants to fund lies in first defining their value to us. Everything costs something. Buying a faster aircraft has a price tag. Moving across the country for a new job also has economic, relational and emotional costs. Again, everything costs something. Value means getting benefits that are worth more to you than the costs. If a $50K aircraft will bring your life greater benefits than that money in the bank or invested in something else, then it has a value greater than the cost. If owning and flying a $50K airplane means you're going to have to sell other valuable assets, take a second job and miss out on some other priceless things in life, then maybe it doesn't have sufficient value to you. Value is as subjective as is setting a flying budget.

This seemingly is common sense. But we have all gotten over our heads at some point trying to define the difference between need and want – and assessing value. So a frugal pilot periodically reviews flying goals and plans looking for what will offer the best value: benefits greater than the cost. By looking at each purchase, upgrade, training and other aviation transactions as an opportunity to seek the best value, we can fund more fun flying.

Let's talk about how safety fits into the aviation equation. Once we buy a plane and/or get a license, safety is a necessary part of flying. It's a need. Flying may or may not be a personal need for you (though my guess is: yes), but once the decision to fly is made, safety is as critical as fuel. You don't want to just fly an airplane, you want a safe airplane. Frugal pilots aren't cheap or unsafe; they seek value for every dollar spent. That means safety is a vital need. For example, replacing worn tires comes before an instrument or interior upgrade. Finish that annual inspection before shopping for goodies. Spend some money on mountain aviation training before planning a long trip over a mountain range.

Frugal pilots can get more things on their wants list by shopping for value. Rather than just writing a check, they do a little research first to make sure that value is greater than price. Here are some examples:

Keep a wish list at your favorite airplane parts supplier's website and make purchases on long-term needs when the total or a special promotion offers free shipping.

Ask your pilot friends for recommendations on services, parts, medical exams, fuel and anything else you buy to fly.

Use the power of the Internet to search for recommendations and pricing.

If possible, delay large purchases for a few weeks or even months to analyze whether it will be a need or an impulse buy.

If you are upgrading instruments or other parts, resell the replaced parts (in good working order) through Trade-a-Plane, eBay, aviation clubs or to local pilots.

Ask your favorite mechanic if you can assist with the annual inspection and any necessary repairs. Even simple jobs like removing the interior and inspection plates can save the mechanic time and your money – and teach you more about your aircraft. (More on this topic in the next column.)

If you rent your wings, ask about prepayment discounts. Buying blocks of rental time can save you money.

The bottom line here is value: getting more than you pay for. It works for buying a house, shopping for groceries or flying an airplane. It's what makes you a frugal pilot.

Be Smart About Aircraft Maintenance

One things all airplanes need is regular maintenance, even ones that don't fly much. A frugal pilot knows how much of that maintenance he or she can legally do and comfortably do. What preventive maintenance an owner-pilot can legally do on an aircraft is outlined in FAR Part 43. In summary, you can service tires, landing gear struts, wheel bearings, and do some lubrication, make simple fabric and fairing patches, replenish hydraulic fluids, replace seats and safety belts, do simple landing-light maintenance, replace and gap spark plugs, replace non-hydraulic hose connections, clean or replace fuel and oil filters and service or replace batteries. Anything else requires direct supervision or work by a certified aircraft mechanic. Read Part 43 Appendix A (c) before starting. It also requires that you make powerplant and/or airframe log entries with a description of the work, date of completion and the name of the person doing the work. A certified mechanic will add their A&P certificate number; you as the aircraft's registered owner or co-owner will include your pilot certificate number.

Your maintenance comfort-level depends on how you feel about working on machines. If you're okay with changing your car's oil and filter and driving it afterwards, you'll probably be comfortable with many of the allowed maintenance jobs an owner-p lot can do. Even so, it's frugal to have an aircraft mechanic show you how to do it on your aircraft the first time. Take pictures and make notes. It may be months or a year or more before you do it yourself.

One of the primary advantages to doing your own aircraft maintenance – besides saving money to buy more fuel – is that you will more intimately know your plane. You'll feel more confident flying it, especially on cross-country trips where you're leaving the comfort of your home nest and mechanic behind. Also, it will make your preflight inspection more meaningful as you understand how systems work and what the signs are that indicate they might not.

Aircraft maintenance, just like maintenance on any machine, can extend its life – or at least let it live a full and productive life. No one can fully predict how long an aircraft engine will last, no more than a doctor can give a newborn a guarantee of a specific number of years of life. But by taking care of ourselves and our aircraft and other machines, we can get more value from them.

FAR Part 43 also outlines what is required for your aircraft's annual or 100-hour inspection. Before your next inspection, read it and determine if there are some of the jobs you can or want to do either prior to or during your mechanic's inspection. Many of us frugal pilots seek out qualified mechanics who allow owner-assisted annuals. We often save a little money, but we also get a valuable education. And we have a professional watching over us to make sure we get that new safety wire on correctly.

Another consideration in aircraft engine maintenance is TBO or time-between-overhaul. It certainly isn't a guarantee of a specific number of hours of service. It's the manufacturer's estimate of how long the typical engine that is run under normal operating conditions will probably last. Typical – normal –

probably. Soft qualifiers that suggest that it's really just an educated guess. They don't know you, how you fly, how dutiful you are about maintenance and the skill level of the various mechanics you hire or the quality of parts you buy. Nor does the manufacturer know if you'll be flying your plane 25 hours a year or 250. So you'll hear about 1800-hour TBO engines that fail in the first 100 hours and others that have flown 2500 or more hours and still have compression in the high 70s. The TBO is just one small indicator of engine condition.

What you can count on is that engines that get more use, such as 100+ hours a year, typically (there's that soft qualifier again) last longer than those that only fly a couple dozen hours a year. That's because metal corrosion can cause more problems than wear. And quality preventive maintenance – your plane doesn't care whether it's you or a well-paid mechanic – can extend the useful life of an engine and airframe.

A frugal pilot can help maintain and even repair his or her aircraft. Saving money is part of the reason. More important is learning about the aircraft, how it works and how to avoid it not working.

Learn from Your Experiences

Every owner-pilot should have a Frugal Notebook. It's a blank book you can keep in the glove box or your flight bag to record things about your airplane. If you are a renter, it's a handy place to record your experiences with specific aircraft and flying conditions. Let's take a look at a few of the things your Frugal Notebook can help with.

Maintenance: Your Frugal Notebook is a good location to make notes on possible maintenance issues as your "squawk list." Record equipment issues as or soon after they occur. Review your latest notes as part of your preflight inspection and postflight review to determine if there is anything that should ground you. In between flights, do a little more research to see if the squawk is something you can fix or it needs a mechanic, making notes in your Frugal Notebook. Use the notebook to record part numbers, vendors, costs and anything else that will help you maintain your aircraft as airworthy and safe.

Oil Changes: Oil is your aircraft engine's blood supply. It not only keeps moving parts lubricated, it also helps keep the engine cooler by transferring some of the heat from the cylinders to the oil cooler or oil pan. Changing oil and filter – whether you do it or a mechanic does it – is a cost-effective way to keep the engine's blood healthy. It also offers an opportunity for a blood test: an engine oil analysis. By getting an analysis at every oil change (typically about $25) you can make historical comparisons to determine whether the engine is producing metals that indicate specific wear problems. If you are trying out a recommended oil additive, you can record when it was added and what the results were. All this gets recorded in your Frugal Notebook.

Leaning: Adjusting the fuel-air mixture, leaning, is important to fuel economy and engine life. For engines built to run on 87-octane that must now use 100LL, leaning is especially important to reduce the chances of excess lead fowling the spark plugs. But just how much should you lean your engine and when? During climb? At higher altitude airports or flights? How much during cruise and descent? Are there exceptions? The answers to these vital questions come from experience – your experience – and the recommendations of the manufacturer. Some POHs offer specific guidance on when and how much to lean the fuel-air mixture. Others are very general. If your POH is specific, record best practices in your Frugal Notebook along with your own observations. If guidance is general, use your next few flights to experiment with leaning to determine what settings give you the greatest power and efficiency. Some aircraft suggest "adjust the mixture control for best power by pulling the knob out until the RPM decreases slightly, then push the control knob forward to maximum RPM. Readjust for each change in power, altitude or with carburetor heat." Record your observations in your Frugal Notebook.

> **Frugal Tip**: I keep a sticky note in my cockpit that reminds me of the tach time or date for specific events such as next oil & filter, transponder check, annual inspection, ELT battery replacement, registration, medical certificate and flight review. It saves me time wondering whether I am up-to-date.

Spending: Most pilots keep two sets of books: double-entry bookkeeping. One set is for the spouse who asks what you've spent on flying. The other set is the actual amount you spent. Your Frugal Notebook is an excellent place to keep track of your actual flying expenses. Besides recording purchases, it can be used for analysis and observation such as how much fuel you purchased last year, how much you spent on maintenance versus repairs, etc. Periodic review of your aviation spending can help you get more value for your dollars – the goal of any frugal pilot. It also can help you document any tax-deductible expenses for your aircraft and flying.

Flying: Your Frugal Notebook is also a handy location to make notes on your flying experiences. It could be a travelogue if you wish. Or it can simply be a place to record favorite airports as well as places to which you wouldn't return. Such records can help you choose places to fly to in the future. "Where was the airstrip next to that historic old town in Oregon?" "Next flight into this area, let's see what's at that little airport to the north." Reviewing your flying notes during the winter can help you plan your upcoming flying season better.

Keeping a Frugal Notebook shouldn't be a chore. It's an opportunity to document and review what you like about flying as well as what it takes to be safe and proficient. It can help you make common-sense decisions toward getting good value from every flying activity and dollar. And that's what being a frugal pilot is all about.

Learn from Smarter Pilots

We pilots typically don't like to admit it, but some pilots are smarter than we are – at least on some topics. The aim of the frugal pilot is to learn something useful from more experienced pilots and aircraft owners. Here are my suggestions on how to get good answers:

Ask Good Questions

Sometimes the most difficult part of getting a good answer is figuring out what the best question is. Rather than "What oil should I buy?" a better question may be "How would you advise me to select the best quality oil and filter for my high-time Piper Arrow?" Ask a specific rather than an open-ended question for best results.

Once you've framed the question, consider how to approach another pilot with it. If you want a variety of opinions, offer the clarified question to pilots at your next hangar flying event, social get-together or weekend congregation. For better results, select one or two pilots (see below) and get them into the frame of offering valuable counsel by prefacing your question with something like "I need some help with an aviation question and would really appreciate your advice." That approach appreciates the listener's experience and asks him or her to treat your question with an open mind and best knowledge.

Be Selective

As your flying experience expands, you learn to recognize who are the better pilots. It may be found in what they say, but more often in what they do. Many pilots talk a good flying experience, but flying with them can tell more than any conversation. Do you seem to have the same approach to flying? Would you invite one pilot-friend over another on a cross-country with you? These are the pilots whose knowledge and skills about flying you most respect. These are the pilots who are as smart, maybe even smarter on some subjects than yourself. And they have different experiences from which they have learned. They have something to teach you.

If you're an aircraft owner, you've met others who have more experience with aircraft ownership, maintenance and repairs than you. Maybe you envy their aircraft and the condition they keep it in. Or they have experience in one or two areas where you could use their advice: upgrading instruments, selecting a STOL aircraft or kit, or finding a good mechanic who encourages owner-assisted annual inspections. Identify and note these owner-pilots and their expertise in your Frugal Notebook.

Most pilots join several different aviation clubs and associations over the years, but soon find one or two that focus on their type of flying and approach to aviation. These are the groups in which you would consider a lifetime membership. Maybe it's a brand or model club, a state or regional group, or an association that focuses on aspects of pleasure or business aviation. These are your sources of knowledge, the pilots and advisors who have their own unique experiences from which they have learned valuable lessons.

Listen Well

You've framed a great question and asked it of a knowledgeable person. But maybe the answer isn't coming out clearly. The question wasn't heard the way you thought it would be. Or maybe the listener didn't understand the terms you used. Time to clarify. "Sorry, but what I meant to say was..." Carefully, you can guide the conversation toward an answer that better fits what you need to know.

Once you have a practical answer from your resource, write it in your Frugal Notebook. As you do so, additional questions may crop up and you can get answers or clarifications while you still have your resource nearby. And remember to thank your advisor for helping you.

What does all this have to do with being a frugal pilot? A frugal pilot is one who makes common-sense decisions toward getting good value from every flying activity and dollar. Some of those decisions are based on what you've learned about flying. They can be enhanced by learning valuable lessons from the experiences of other pilots. The bottom line is: To get a valuable answer, ask a good question of someone who knows.

One more tip: Be a valuable resource to other pilots. Answer clarified questions with as much helpful guidance as you would like other pilots to offer you. Clearly differentiate between what you know as fact and what your experience has developed as opinion. And don't be concerned if the listener doesn't take your advice. Frugal pilots recognize that there are many ways of doing the same thing well.

Shop Smarter

You know the quip: What makes an airplane fly? *Money!* Sometimes, it seems, lots of money!

But aviation isn't the only money-hungry pastime. Just about every component of life costs money, sometimes lots of money. So, how can we, as pilots – as consumers – get good value while spending less money? By shopping smarter.

Analyze Needs and Wants

As we discussed in an earlier column, being a Frugal Pilot (or Frugal Anything) means first separating needs and wants. Remember: At the grocery store, a *need* is buying milk, bread and other food staples. A *want* is getting soda, corn chips and snack cakes. In recreational aviation, a *need* is something required to meet your flying goals and your budget. A *want* is not required but desired. Wants aren't bad things. They're just not as critical to aviation safety as needs. So prioritizing our needs and wants is the first step in shopping smarter.

Determine Value

The best way to prioritize the things we buy is by first determining their value toward reaching our goals. How much value will that new GPS-gadget add to our safety and enjoyment of flying? Is there another unit that will give us as much value for a lower price? Is a used or refurbished unit a good option or is it false economy? Remember that a frugal pilot is not a cheap pilot. Nor is a frugal pilot unsafe. A frugal pilot is one who makes common-sense decisions toward getting good value from every flying activity and dollar.

Seek Discounts

If you do any kind of shopping, you've noticed that the same product can be sold by many retailers and nearly as many different prices. MSRP is the Manufacturer's Suggested Retail Price and retailers often use it as a starting point for discounts to attract customers.

Some manufacturers don't allow much if any discounting on more unique products such as those we pilots buy. However, there still are discounts available, even if it is free shipping or a satisfaction guarantee. Other retailers offer discounts who make more or larger purchases such as Frequent Buyer programs. Or their ads say "Call us first for the lowest price." Still other sellers have daily, weekly, or monthly deals that can save you money on what you want.

Be Ready to Buy

Smart shoppers avoid impulse buying, but once they have chosen a quality product to buy they stay ready to buy, watching for the best deal. That means getting watching publication ads (like GAN), getting on aviation retailer email lists for specials and making sure the funds are set aside for smart purchases.

Of course, not all aviation purchases can wait for a SALE. But by analyzing your flying needs and wants, and determining value, you can make better purchase decisions in a hurry as well. You may not get the best price ever, but you can get the best price now.

Ask

Sometimes the best way to get the best price is to ask for it. Give the seller a reason to give you a discount, such as: You are my favorite aviation retailer, I've purchased all of my avionics/supplies/books from you, or I'm on a budget and could use a discount. It's best to first identify who may have discount authority and ask that person. Make that person feel good about offering you a good deal.

If you're buying something bigger, like an airplane, prices aren't always set in stone and discounts or price reductions are expected. Again, ask. If you don't feel comfortable negotiating, ask one of your friends or relatives who is to help you with the purchase. You can sometimes determine a "typical" discount offered by a seller by analyzing the asking-versus-final prices on prior sales.

Do Your Homework

Another technique for shopping for aircraft is to thoroughly do your homework. Find out what similar aircraft are selling for, determine if there are any STCs that you will have to face as the new owner. Look for any information than can help you impress the seller that you are a knowledgeable buyer who wants value. Shop smarter.

Shopping smarter can work for anything you buy. The advantage it offers to aviation consumers is that every dollar you save is another dollar you can spend on avgas! Fly more and spend less as a frugal pilot.

Barter and Trade

If your flying budget is tight, like mine is, there are many ways to cut your flying costs without spending a lot of money. You can borrow, rent, trade or barter for some of the things you need. Not everything aviation can be exchanged this way, but there are some – and each can save you money to buy more fun-fuel.

Rent or Borrow

Let's start the list with aircraft. Many frugal pilots determine that they just don't fly enough to justify buying a plane for flying 1% of a year – about 80 hours. Renting makes much more sense, especially if they can get a discount by pre-paying for aircraft time, called "blocks." Ask your aircraft rental resource about this.

Other frugal pilots get enough flight hours to own, but still want to fly something different once in a while: a four-seater for a family trip, an IFR aircraft to stay current, a tail-dragger or aerobatic aircraft just for fun. In many cases, an owner of one of these aircraft could be talked into letting you borrow their wings, as long as you meet their skill requirements and maybe trade time in your aircraft or trade for another asset. I've been approached by a number of aircraft owners who will let me fly their wings for the price of fuel and a promise to keep the dirty side down. There's a check-out ride involved, but you may know of a few pilots who will let you borrow.

Trade Assets

You have a wide variety of assets besides cash. These assets can be traded for what you want. For example, you can exchange your goods or services for someone else's goods or services. That's called bartering. It's similar to a cash transaction without the cash.

The most obvious place to start a trade is by listing out what you have that you can trade. Then make a list of what aviation things (aircraft, flight time, parts, fuel, services) that you need. Finally, begin looking at your aviation buddies for folks who have what you need and need what you have. For example, a student pilot who builds websites as a job traded a flight school for a new website in exchange for instruction. Another pilot traded a used car for an annual inspection. One pilot traded hangar rent for airport repairs.

Barter and Trade Resources

If you've never done much bartering or trading, you may be surprised at how much is being done. The U.S. barter economy is estimated at over $12 Billion-with-a-B a year. No currency exchanges hands. In tough economic times, that number goes up. Here are some resources for getting into the barter-and-trade economy with your aviation needs.

GeneralAviationNews.com and the print version of GAN include many classified ads with the word "trade" in them. Trade up, trade down.

Trade-A-Plane.com includes numerous aircraft available for trade. In most cases, the trade is asset-for-asset rather than service-for-asset.

GoSwap.org is an online property barter site that includes land, houses, cars, boats, aircraft and other larger assets. There is a fee for listings, but you can read the Search results for free and look for something you want.

TradeAway.com is a listing service for barter transactions including transportation (cars, motorcycles, aircraft).

Craigslist.org is the grand-daddy of whatever-you-got transactions. It one of the top 50 websites in the world! Select the edition for your area and Search for "aircraft" and "trade" or "barter" and be amazed. Also, be careful. Because it is so popular, it has been abused and there are numerous scams. Remember: "If it sounds too good to be true, it probably is."

Even bigger than craigslist is **eBay.com**. At any given time, more than 500 million items are for sale on eBay including aircraft, parts, books and avionics. (I purchased my Cessna 150 via eBay!) And there are 128 million buyers and sellers using the system. Barter and trade are not so easy on eBay, but it is a good resource for selling assets you don't need and getting good-old-cash for them.

One caveat: Barter and trade transactions are subject to taxation, just as are cash transactions. U.S. laws say that such transactions are supposed to be reported to the IRS on Form 1099-B, *Proceeds from Broker and Barter Exchange Transactions*. Your state or municipality may have similar requirements.

Here's a good option for the frugal pilot: Consider bartering or trading the next time you reach for your flying wallet. Fly more and spend less.

Multitask Flying

The retail price of avgas continues to climb with fewer refineries supplying it. Aircraft parts, never cheap, increase in cost each year as new-old stock dwindles. Smaller airports close and larger airports raise hangar rents. Fewer private pilots are flying today than ten years ago, reducing economy of scale. Flying is getting too dang expensive.

However, flying remains an unrivaled pastime. Flying literally offers a third dimension over two-dimensional recreation such as boating, motorcycling, and RVing.

Flying also offers opportunities for multi-purposing: combine a business trip and vacation, practice slow dutch rolls on a long flight, use a pleasure trip to practice for an upcoming flight review. Flying challenges and rewards. Frugal pilots discover new ways to reduce the costs and increase the joy of flying. One of the ways is by combining flight goals. Here are some suggestions.

Flying for Pleasure

Many pilots fly because it is <u>not</u> related to what they do during the weekday. Pilots I know work in lumber mills, operate a pharmacy, run a back-hoe business, engineer a train, publish newspapers, work in city government, and are retired civil servants. For some, flying is their release from the stresses of their day job. For others, flying is a controlled adrenalin boost.

Most private pilots fly primarily for fun. We seek the best hundred-dollar hamburger, attend fly-ins, fly to vacations, and inspect clouds. But we sometimes get into a rut, flying to the same airport grease-shack each Saturday or flying the same loop to the same airports once a fortnight.

Frugal pilots discover new ways to fly for pleasure. They offer a ride to anyone who will buy them lunch and maybe chip in for fuel. They take their boss up for a flight to improve work relationships. They take friends to a fly-in for the cost of fuel. They repay social debts by offering airplane rides. Frugal pilots find ways of covering flying expenses and increasing the fun.

Adding Business to Flying

Many pleasure pilots find business reasons to help pay for their flying. They buy and sell aviation parts or related products on Barnstormers or eBay or at fly-ins. They use their private aircraft to attend professional conferences. They fly people or packages that their employers need urgently delivered. The IRS allows fuel and other aviation costs as legitimate expenses for people who have established a for-profit business, no matter how small. Of course, pilots flying for business must obey FAA requirements regarding a commercial pilot license.

Flying for Training

To remain proficient, pilots need on-going training and experience. Frugal pilots don't have to stop what they're doing to perform training. They can multitask and improve flight proficiency while flying for other reasons. If flying for pleasure with an experienced pilot, they can practice unusual attitude recovery. Flying with a more experienced pilot offers an opportunity to learn advanced techniques from another aviator.

Flying for whatever reason offers opportunities to practice takeoffs and landings you typically don't do: simulated short field and soft field. You also can take a few minutes at your destinat on airport to practice a few landings.

Flying for business or pleasure also offers you time to review and practice safety procedures. Pull out your Emergency Checklist and review what to do if there is an engine fire on the ground or in flight, a cockpit fire, an engine loss on takeoff, engine loss during flight, a rough-running engine, high oil temperature, or other potential in-flight problems. Go through the motions, checking instruments and identifying the steps needed to resolve the emergency. There may be a day soon that you will be tested. Meantime, you will be building confidence in yourself and your aircraft.

Another procedure to practice from time to time is the emergency descent. As you are nearing a familiar airport, perform a forward slip of your aircraft to descend at 1000 fpm or more. Caution: Don't try this with passengers without letting them know first and making sure that they will be comfortable. Call the practice off immediately if any passenger is uncomfortable.

There are many ways that a frugal pilot can expand aviation horizons while reducing flying costs. Frugal pilots know that multitasking their flying is a practical way to get more fun for less money. That's what frugal flying is all about!

Staying Frugal

For many private pilots, renting makes more sense than buying an airplane. The ongoing costs of compliance, maintenance, and storage added to the rising costs of fuel can bring the hourly cost of flying your own aircraft within the range of renting one.

Rent to Fly

In some cases, it works; in others, not. The availability of well-maintained rental aircraft in your area may be extensive, limited, or even non-existent. You may discover your near-perfect wings at a nearby airport and buy a discounted block of rental time to save money. Or you may have to drive an hour each way just to fly for an hour. Or local FBOs may not rent the type of aircraft you want to fly.

Or you may just decide that renting someone else's wings doesn't make flying as much fun for you. Maybe you'll decide to pay a premium to fly your own aircraft over one that is rented to every Orville and Wilbur with a license to fly.

Prequalified Rentals

One of the problems faced by aircraft renters is that they typically have to get a checkride with the FBO before scheduling their first rental. Depending on the renter, the pilot may need a checkride in each plane that the pilot wants to rent, especially if the pilot has under 300 hours on the log. It makes sense as the renter is giving keys to a large investment for a relatively small fee.

OpenAirplane.com (not an endorsement) serve as a middle-man between renters and rentees, prequalifying the rental aircraft and potential renters. A renter can earn a Universal Pilot Checkout to make credential verification easier and either reduce or eliminate the need for a checkride before rental at airports throughout the country.

On the other side of the transaction, owners of rental aircraft can list their inventory as available and include costs and requirements. Rental aircraft can be owned by individuals, partnerships, FBOs, flight schools, or flying clubs. The service brings the renter and rentee together as well as manages the liability insurance. Their fee is paid by the renter.

Decisions, Decisions

Renting vs. owning is a Frugal Pilot Decision that only you can make as your situation is relatively unique. You may only want to fly high-performance aircraft on long trips, or ultralights above the tree-tops, or a classic light-sport aircraft to regional fly-ins, or an experimental aircraft that you built. In all cases, you can apply the principles of Frugal Flying to your decisions. As outlined in the past nine columns of *The Frugal Pilot*, they include: remember why you fly, keep it simple, manage your needs and wants, learn from your experiences, learn from smarter pilots, shop smarter, barter and trade, and multitask your flying.

The most important takeaway is that a Frugal Pilot is not a cheap pilot. Nor is a Frugal Pilot unsafe. A Frugal Pilot is one who makes common-sense decisions toward getting good value from every flying activity and dollar. Fly more and spend less as a Frugal Pilot.

Advanced Frugal Flying

Frugal Pilots have additional options for funding their fun. It makes good sense for many pilots who fly less than a 100 hours a year to consider what are broadly known as partnerships or flying clubs. The fixed costs of aircraft, maintenance, and storage are reduced. Only the cost of fuel burned remains the same. Let's get more specific.

Co-ownership typically includes two or three pilots who all have their names on an aircraft registration. Obviously, co-owners are selected for their personal and aviation compatibility, an option not typically available to FBO aircraft renters. Co-ownerships make sense for pilots of less-expensive simpler aircraft.

Partnerships can be of any number, but practically have three to five members. The legal structure is a little more complex than a co-ownership, as it should be with more folks involved. The insurance policy is more expensive than for a single pilot, but not prohibitive. For a majority of pilots who want to fly a more expensive aircraft, a partnership makes good sense.

Flying Clubs can be of any size, but usually involve two or more aircraft and six or more members. As you can imagine, aviation liability insurance at this level becomes much more complex and expensive. With opportunities come intricacies and smart flying clubs have worked out all the bugs over the years so that members can focus on what they love the most: frugal flying.

Are one of these options right for you? Maybe. In the next few chapters, I'll include articles on how you can partner with other pilots to dramatically reduce the costs of flying with co-ownerships, partnerships, and flying clubs.

Sharing Your Wings

For many frugal pilots, sharing their wings makes lots of sense. Most private pilots fly less than 1% of the available hours in a year, often not enough time to keep their aircraft from suffering from inactivity. Add another pilot or two and the plane actually stays in better condition – and the costs go down.

But the big question isn't so much should you share your wings, but how. Obviously, it's not a thorough analogy, but sharing wings is something like sharing a life in marriage: the partnership can either be twice as good or twice as bad as going it alone.

Making the Decision

Sharing your wings – or not – is an important decision. Your answers to these and related questions are dynamic and may change over the next few years as your flying goals, resources, and friendships change. So, it's best to take a long-term look at your flying world before making a decision that will impact many aspects of your life, ideally for the better.

Making a decision to share your wings requires answering a few important questions:

- ✓ Why should I share? (reduce costs, aircraft utilization, friendship, tax advantages)

- ✓ What should I share? (two-seat simple aircraft, four-seat aircraft with luggage capacity, IFR aircraft, an LSA, a variety of airplanes)

- ✓ How should I share? (simple agreement with a friend, formal partnership contract, form a non-profit corporation)

- ✓ Who should I share with? (best friends, thousand-hour pilots, other students)

- ✓ What are my flying resources? (how much money can I invest, what is my monthly budget, what other resources can I draw on?)

Flying Goals

Sharing wings works best if all partners agree on common flying goals, the WHY. The answer dictates what type of aircraft will be shared, how it will be used, and how happy the members potentially will be with the partnership.

For example, four pilots all with similar flying goals and experiences can probably develop a mutually-satisfying long-term flying relationship. But if two of the pilots immediately want to start upgrading avionics and the two others don't, there could be immediate conflict and problems. An honest discussion among potential partners before anything is agreed to or purchased, can make the partnership stronger. Think of this period as the courtship.

Structure

An aviation partnership requires four elements:

- • Compatible members

- Appropriate aircraft
- Workable structure
- Responsible management

Even before selecting an airplane, a critical question to sharing wings is: With who? Again, like a marriage, the right partnership can make aviation more enjoyable. Compatibility is the key. Not only do your partners need to have similar flying goals, but also well-matched personalities. You don't have to all be brothers/sisters from another mother, but you do need to agree on how to disagree. The WHO leads to the HOW and WHAT.

There are many ways of structuring a relationship around aircraft owning and flying. As summarized in my last column – and developed in future columns – the most common structures include:

- Co-ownership
- Partnership
- Flying clubs

Each has its advantages and disadvantages, to be discussed along with options and recommended terms of agreement. Depending on group size, flying goals, and assets, a simple agreement may be sufficient. Flying clubs may prefer to have a non-profit charter of incorporation or other structure that fits the flying goals of its members.

Insurance Questions

Aviation insurance is a component of sharing wings that often doesn't get discussed until the relationship is formed. Sometimes that's too late. Talk over your aircraft sharing arrangement ideas with an experienced aviation insurance broker before making a decision.

Why? Because aviation insurers will base your group premiums on factors that you should know about before you get too serious. For example, aviation insurance premiums often are based on the least experienced member of the group, such as a student or newly-minted pilot. The rates may not go up very much, but the partnership should be aware of higher premiums and plan accordingly. Maybe the student must pay a little more for group membership until hours are built.

Another insurance issue is based on the number of pilots in your group. Some insurers consider a partnership of six or more pilots a commercial flying club (higher rates) than a partnership or co-ownership. This condition may suggest that you limit your group's size – or shop for another insurer with broader definitions of what a commercial policy requires. These and other insurance questions will be discussed further in future columns, but it's a good idea to be thinking about them now as you first consider sharing your wings.

Co-Ownership Decisions

You've decided to *consider* sharing your wings. Good for you! Like sharing a life, sharing an asset can benefit numerous people and allow them to potentially do more than going it alone. But it also can complicate life. Making a logical decision about co-ownership can help you get more for your flying investment.

Co-Ownership and the FAA

A co-ownership is the simplest way to share wings. Basically, it puts two or more names on the aircraft title and establishes an agreement on how to allocate an asset. A partnership, covered in a future column, is more complex and often is used for sharing business aircraft or at least where more money or partners is involved.

To establish an aircraft co-ownership, all you really need is a simple agreement and an update to the aircraft's FAA registration. To register an aircraft, send an Aircraft Registration Application (AC Form 8050-1), a bill of sale (AC Form 8050-2) or other evidence of ownership, and the $5 registration fee to the FAA Aircraft Registration Branch. The forms and additional instructions are available from your regional FSDO.

The Agreement

The agreement between co-owners can be as simple as a handshake or as complex as you want an attorney to make it. Most co-owners agree to something in between: a written and signed agreement outlining rights and responsibilities of the participants. This column and the next one will cover many of the things you should consider when establishing a co-ownership agreement.

One of the most important questions of co-ownership answers what happens to the asset, the airplane, if one of the partners dies. Do the other partners get the plane? The person's beneficiaries? A charity? No one likes to think about these things, but they could become vital questions. Most aircraft co-ownership agreements are considered **tenancy-in-common**, meaning that ownership passes to the dead co-owner's beneficiaries. If the agreement is a **joint tenancy**, the share goes to the co-owners. Some agreements include a life insurance policy on all co-owners.

Who actually owns the shared aircraft(s)? In a co-ownership or partnership, all the pilots own the aircraft in shares as described in the agreement. In a flying club, to be discussed in a future column, either the organization itself owns the aircraft or possibly an investor who leases it to the club. Make sure your agreement spells this out and covers liability issues.

Sharing Costs

The **initial cost** of the aircraft is the first consideration in a co-ownership agreement. Maybe a group member has an aircraft that will be shared. Or the group will equally divide the cost of an aircraft they will purchase together. This, of course, should be a part of the co-ownership agreement, spelling out the initial investment. If financing is required for one or more co-owners, terms of the financing should be discussed and included in writing.

Fixed costs for co-ownership include group financing, property taxes, hangar or tie-down rental fees, insurance, estimated cost of the annual inspection and other expenses to be paid whether the aircraft flies or not.

Operating costs are the expenses required by flying. They include fuel, oil, engine (oil and filter change) and airframe maintenance, avionics maintenance, etc. Typically, these are charged to the individual co-owners for the number of hours the actually flew during a period, with an annual review and adjustment.

Reserves should be discussed by the group and agreed upon. Typically, this means does the group want to set aside a specific amount (into an escrow fund) to cover propeller and/or engine replacement. These are major expenses, especially on more complex aircraft. For example, if an 1,800-hour-TBO engine now has 600 hours on it and the overhaul would be about $12,000, does the group want to set aside $10-per-flight-hour in a reserve to pay for it. Or does the group take the chance and split the expense if and when necessary. Best to work this out in advance in your co-ownership agreement.

Typically, co-ownership agreements outline how the costs are covered. Fixed expenses, the costs of <u>owning</u> the aircraft, usually are shared equally among co-owners. Operating costs and any reserves, the costs of <u>flying</u> the aircraft, are shared based on the number of hours flown by individuals. A monthly bill for each co-owner is calculated and paid, either as a formal invoice or across the table at a monthly owner's meeting.

Sharing Aircraft

You also need to spell out how the aircraft will be shared among the co-owners. Does someone with a larger share get priority?

Do some co-owners get weekend priority? What if one of the co-owners takes the aircraft out of town for a while? Will there be a flight log in the aircraft for recording flights? How will the questions about liability be resolved? These and many other questions need to be discussed and answered early in the relationship to ensure that the relationship will last.

Writing A Co-Ownership Agreement

The previous article of *The Frugal Pilot* covered the advantages and disadvantages of aircraft co-ownership toward helping you decide whether fractional ownership is right for you. This article will assume that you've decided to share your wings and cover the things you will want in your written co-ownership agreement.

Get It in Writing

A co-ownership agreement is a simple document between two to four people who want to share an aircraft. It doesn't need all the whereases and heretofores required by a partnership or flying club. In fact, it doesn't even have to be in writing. However, getting the agreement in writing will help minimize communication problems that typically crop up. As the relationship continues, it's a good idea to periodically review the original agreement terms – and that's easier if they are in writing.

Disclaimer: I am *not* a lawyer. However, I have written many simple legal agreements that have stood the test of time and legal battles. My legal philosophy is never to write a contract with someone you don't trust. Following is a sample co-ownership agreement.

A Simple Agreement

This agreement between Joe Smith and John Doe (co-owners), dated September 15, 2014, is for the purpose of acquiring a 1970 Wingaling (N12345) and holding the title thereto as Tenants in Common. The purchase price shall be $20,000, of which one-half (1/2) or $10,000, shall be paid in cash equally by the co-owners.

Base: The aircraft shall be based at the Rutabaga Airport and the costs of hangar or tie-down there shall be borne equally by the co-owners. Costs of storage or landing fees while the aircraft is operated away from the base airport shall be borne by the co-owner so operating.

Fixed Costs: Fixed expenses include hangar or tie-down rental fees, insurance, estimated cost of the annual inspection, group financing, and property taxes. A Fixed Expense account shall be maintained and contributed to equally by the partners. The contribution rate shall be $100.00 per co-owner per month, adjusted periodically as required to cover anticipated expenses.

Operating Costs: Operating expenses include fuel, oil, engine and airframe maintenance, avionics maintenance, and related maintenance. All operating expenses shall be paid out of this fund and shared based on the hours the aircraft was flown by each co-owner. [Alternately: The contribution rate shall be $100.00 per co-owner per month, adjusted periodically as required to cover anticipated expenses.]

Insurance: Adequate insurance shall be carried by the co-owners to insure against the reasonably anticipated risk of the operations intended. The person operating the aircraft when subject to an insurance claim shall pay the policy deductible.

Authorized Pilots: No other person other than the co-owners shall be authorized to operate the aircraft except with the express consent of all co-owners, and then only if that person has the experience level required by the aircraft's insurance policy.

Usage: No commercial or for-hire operations, as defined by current FAA regulations, may be performed in the aircraft. No flight instruction activities, except as required by the co-owners to maintain or upgrade their current certification, may be performed in the aircraft.

Flight Scheduling: The aircraft shall be available on a first-come, first-served basis as recorded on the Flight Scheduling Sheet in the aircraft.

Flight Log: All flights shall be recorded immediately after each flight on the Flight Log in the aircraft. The Flight Log shall include entries for identified maintenance or repair issues.

Responsibilities: It is agreed that Joe Smith will manage the financial records and John Doe will manage the maintenance records for this co-ownership, each keeping the other informed on status at any time requested.

Expanding the Agreement

Depending on what level of formality the co-owners want, a simple agreement can be expanded to include additional conditions and guidelines. For example, if you agree that the engine, propeller, or airframe will soon need some major work in the near future, you can establish a reserve account that anticipates the cost. Or you can simply wait until it's needed and work out equal sharing of costs.

Scheduling flying time in your shared wings may be more complex than a sheet in the cockpit. You can use one of the online flight scheduling programs available, such as

AircraftClubs.com, FlightSchedulePro.com, PilotSchedule.com, or SkyManager.com.

If there is a concern about ownership in the case of the death of one of the co-owners, put something in your agreement that solves the problem. Same for concerns about liability. If one or both the partners are concerned that a partner could be incur liability beyond what the agreement covers, then add a clause that clarifies how liability will be handled.

One more resource for those thinking of co-ownership: The AOPA offers an online *Pilot's Guide to Co-Ownership* covering the relevant topics to help you find a long-term way to share your wings.

Partnership Decisions

Aircraft fractional ownership or co-ownership, discussed in the last two articles, is the simplest way for many pilots to cut the costs of flying. Two or three pilots write a simple agreement of how they will share their wings. For a larger group of owners or a more complex or expensive aircraft, an aircraft partnership makes more sense. This article covers the various decisions you and others need to make to have a successful aircraft partnership.

Partnership Basics

A partnership agreement is a more complex document between two or more people who want to share an aircraft. It will include a lot more legalese than a simple co-ownership agreement, but doesn't have to be as thick as the agreement for a flying club. However, you should consult an attorney or at least a paralegal in drawing it up. Partnership Agreement forms available at stationery stores are written for small businesses and won't be appropriate for conditions of an aircraft partnership. Consider good legal counsel an investment rather than an expense. Both the AOPA and EAA offer legal resources to members.

Partnership Agreement

Aviation partnerships typically include three to five partners. A partnership agreement is a written agreement between two or more individuals who join as partners to control assets. The assets, in this case, are one or more aircraft, though most multiple-aircraft partnerships elect to become flying clubs (covered in a later column). The partnership agreement outlines the nature of the relationship, the capital contributed by each partner, and their rights and responsibilities. It also should cover liability issues and that's where a savvy attorney can help. All these elements are included in the "articles of partnership".

- ➢ What should you and your partner(s) decide before you write and sign a partnership agreement?

- ➢ Why do we want to consider sharing an aircraft with another owner? Cost reduction? Friendship? Better aircraft?

- ➢ Where will we find like-minded partners? Friends? Pilot club members? Referrals? Advertise?

- ➢ How reliable are the people being considered for the partnership? Sufficient assets? Dependable? Trustworthy?

- ➢ Must a new partner be voted into the established group unanimously?

- ➢ How much do we want to invest initially and monthly in our flying partnership?

- ➢ How compatible are our individual flying goals?

- ➢ How will we coordinate our individual flying needs?

- ➢ How will we buy fuel and share the costs equitably?

- ➢ How will we take care of aircraft maintenance?

- ➢ Who and how will the partnership pay the bills?

- ➤ How will the aircraft be financed, if required?
- ➤ What will the aircraft partnership cost each member?

Calculating Costs

How much is flying in a partnership going to cost? So many variables need to be considered. The costs of the partnership typically are broken down per-owner and per-flight-hour. Per-owner costs include the divided initial purchase price of the aircraft, the costs of added equipment, and any financing costs plus the ongoing costs of storage, insurance, and depreciation. Per-flight-hour costs include fuel, oil, aircraft and engine maintenance, and engine and propeller overhaul reserves.

Another way of categorizing partnership costs uses:

Initial investment to cover aircraft purchase, any upgrades, and financing costs.

Monthly dues to cover constant expenses such as fixed costs and overhead that don't change often such as hangar rents and insurance.

Hourly rate to cover expenses that change based on flight time such as fuel.

What-If List

After you've gathered a group of like-minded partnership candidates, you can refine your relationship by discussing some of the What-If questions that reveal actual levels of agreement and compatibility. Here are some discussion-starters:

- ➤ What will the partnership do if the engine needs major work?
- ➤ What will the partnership do if the airplane is damaged beyond repair?
- ➤ What happens if a partner dies or loses pilot privileges?

- ➢ What if a partner cannot or will not pay agreed-upon expenses?

- ➢ What if a partner wants or needs to sell his or her share of the assets?

- ➢ What if a partnership dispute requires arbitration?

Creative Partnerships

No two aviation partnerships are exactly alike, just as the partners aren't clones. Many partnerships have developed creative ways of handling unique situations. Here are some examples to consider:

Unequal shares for partners who cannot buy a quarter-share but can afford an eighth-share.

One or more partners agreeing to take a promissory note from another partner for the initial investment.

The partnership agrees to offer a partial share or to reduce monthly dues or hourly rate to a qualified member who does all or a portion of the maintenance or performs some other service for the partnership (legal, financial).

Partners are allowed a two-week block of time each year when the aircraft is exclusively theirs for hunting, vacationing, Oshkosh, or other activities.

From your research and discussion of these issues, you can write an outline of what your partnership agreement should include. This document will save time and money as you have an attorney or paralegal help you produce a workable aviation partnership agreement.

Writing A Partnership Agreement

Now it's time to take off and write the partnership agreement. As a reminder, an aircraft partnership typically can be of any number, but practically has three to five members. The legal structure is a little more complex than a co-ownership, as it should be with more pilots involved. The insurance policy is more expensive than for a single pilot, but not excessive. For a majority of pilots who want to fly a more expensive aircraft than their budget allows, a partnership makes good sense. Flying clubs will be covered in future articles.

The Partnership Agreement

A partnership agreement, also known as Articles of Partnership, is a written agreement between two or more individuals who join as partners to share one or more assets. The asset, in an aviation partnership, is an aircraft. The partnership agreement defines the relationship, the capital contributed by each partner, their rights and responsibilities, and liability issues. It is similar in function to a business partnership, but the agreement is specific to asset management.

Caveat: An aviation partnership agreement should be written up, or at least checked over, by an attorney with aviation experience. You're dealing with an asset worth many thousands of dollars and pilots with hundreds of opinions. Invest in qualified legal counsel.

Articles of Partnership

Components of a typical aviation partnership agreement include clauses (called Articles) covering:

- ➤ Partner Names and Contacts
- ➤ Partnership Purpose
- ➤ Duration of Partnership
- ➤ Partnership Meetings
- ➤ Partnership Rights
- ➤ Partnership Responsibilities
- ➤ Asset(s) Definition
- ➤ Asset(s) Valuation
- ➤ Share Valuation
- ➤ Fixed Expenses
- ➤ Aircraft Insurance
- ➤ Operating Expenses
- ➤ Overhaul and Propeller Funds
- ➤ Accounting
- ➤ Billing and Delinquencies
- ➤ Home Base
- ➤ Usage by Partners
- ➤ Aircraft Scheduling
- ➤ Aircraft Reservations

- ➢ Aircraft Fueling
- ➢ Procedures Away from Home Base
- ➢ Usage by Non-Partner Pilots
- ➢ Aircraft Flight Log
- ➢ Aircraft Maintenance Logs
- ➢ Aircraft Servicing (Squawks)
- ➢ Equipment Upgrades
- ➢ Accident Management
- ➢ Partner Death or Loss of License
- ➢ Partnership Dissolution
- ➢ Arbitration
- ➢ Signatures

To develop a simple outline for your partnership agreement, review the topics and questions outline in the last column of *The Frugal Pilot* (Sept. 20, 2014), Especially focus on the What If questions that can make the difference between a enjoyable partnership and caustic litigation. Also review the Creative Partnership ideas in that article as they can help you develop an everyone-wins aviation venture.

Next, look to sample aviation partnership agreements and sound advice developed by the AOPA, EAA, and other aviation advocate groups. The AOPA, especially, has a variety of resources for pilots considering co-ownership, partnership, or flying clubs.

Once all partner candidates have discussed and verbally agreed to the partnership agreement, it's time to put it on paper. Again, seek legal counsel with aviation experience to review your outline, answer questions, and help all partners feel comfortable with the agreement.

Aircraft Registration

The primary asset, in this case an aircraft, is registered with the FAA either in the names of the individual partners or in a partnership name. It's typically easier to establish and use a partnership name because a change in partners doesn't require a change in FAA records. For example, if Joe Smith buys out Jane Jones' partnership share, the "Flying Fools Partnership" can change the partnership agreement without having to notify the FAA. "Flying Fools Partnership" still owns the aircraft.

If the aircraft or any share of it is financed through a lending institution, it may require notification of the lender if any partners change. Check with your lender to be sure.

Flying Club Decisions

Sharing your wings is a big decision. The goal is to reduce the costs to gain the greatest benefits from flying. Exactly what, how, and why you share your wings offers so many variations and opportunities that there is no single solution. There are many options including co-ownership and partnership. The third option, starting or joining a flying club, offers even more options – and potential problems. Let's take a closer look.

Flying Club Basics

Flying Clubs can be of any size, but usually involve two or more aircraft and six or more members. Sharing wings through a flying club is a good choice for pilots who want access to a variety of aircraft, rather than just one. For example, West Valley Flying Club (wvfc.org) was organized 42 years ago serving pilots in the San Francisco Bay area from two airports. There are more than 40 aircraft in inventory ranging from a Cessna 152 to a Cirrus SR22 with a G1000 glass cockpit. Members pay monthly dues and an hourly rental (wet) for time flown.

The reason why flying clubs need six or more members is that the clubs require a higher level of aviation liability insurance than for a partnership. If you're considering forming a flying club, talk with a few aviation insurance brokers to determine their requirements and comparative costs. Especially important is how many pilots can be on a single policy and at what flying experience levels.

The AOPA reports that there are more than 600 flying clubs in the U.S. That may seem like a lot, but not compared to estimated 4,000 flying clubs in America during the 1960s and 1970s when Cessna was very active in the entry-level aviation market. Also, changes to tax laws regarding aircraft leasebacks – how many flying clubs get their aircraft – has reduced inventory. The AOPA is actively promoting the formation of new flying clubs through their website at AOPA.org/Pilot-Resources/Flying-Clubs.

Types of Flying Club

There are two common types of flying clubs. **Shareholder flying clubs** allow members to purchase a share in the club with their initiation fee and own a percentage of whatever the club jointly buys and owns. **Leaseback flying clubs** use aircraft owned by individuals or corporations and are leased back to the flying club for tax advantages. The type of flying club you form will require expert legal and financial advice – which is why many frugal pilots decide to join an existing flying club rather than start one.

A typical flying club requires many officers, depending on the aircraft inventory and number of members. For example, a larger flying club will include a president, vice president, secretary, treasurer, operations officer, flight safety officer, and a maintenance officer. Smaller clubs will combine some of these jobs. Depending on club structure, the officers may be paid or unpaid.

There's one other type of flying club that is nearly extinct: the FBO flying club. The popular Cessna Flying Clubs of the 1960s and 1970s are these. All of the aircraft are owned by an FBO, in this case an aircraft dealership typically combined with a flight school. Some independent FBOs still operate flying club flight schools, but liability insurance and fewer student pilots has diminished their number over the years.

> **Frugal Tip**: Flight time in most rental aircraft typically is measured with an installed Hobbs Meter, a time instrument that measures how long an aircraft engine operates (based on oil pressure). A tachometer measures engine RPM, so the tach turns slower when taxiing or descending. Engine and other maintenance will be based on tach readings. Many flying clubs use tach time to measure flight duration. Whatever you fly, know which instrument flight time is based on as Hobbs time can be 10-20% higher than tach readings.

How can you find out more about flying clubs in your area? The AOPA Flying Club website mentioned above is an excellent resource. Flying-Club.org offers a listing by state and city. Another resource for flying clubs is SkyManager.com with an integrated software program that helps flying clubs and flight schools smoothly manage all the data and scheduling needed for a successful aviation business.

Flying Club Agreements

Many thousands of frugal pilots continue to fly because of flying clubs. These clubs typically include a wide variety of pilots and at least two aircraft, bringing down the price of going up by sharing the costs of plane ownership and operation. This article continues the discussion with suggestions on how flying club agreements can be structured to meet the needs of a nest of persnickety pilots and aircraft owners.

Flying Club Help

Obviously, a flying club involves more assets, more expenses, and more members than a co-ownership or a partnership of pilots. That's why anyone considering forming a flying club – or even investing in a club membership – should get some legal advice, especially from an attorney with aviation experience. If you have a business attorney, or know someone who can recommend one, start there. Other options include the Lawyer-Pilots Bar Association (lpba.com), the AOPA Legal Services department (aopa.org), and state bar associations.

However, many aviation attorneys specialize in FAA medical resolutions, NTSB aviation accidents and damages, or aviation tax matters. Look for one with experience writing contracts, especially flying club and partnership contracts. If all else fails, use a contracts lawyer and have the documents reviewed by an aviation attorney.

Flying Club Insurance

One of the sticker-shocks of starting a flying club is the cost of insurance. With individual pilots used to paying between $500 and $1,000 a year for aircraft insurance, it seems outrageous to pay that much just for their single share of a flying club membership. Yes, total flying club insurance can be ten times that of an individual pilot's policy.

Why? Because flying club members typically aren't as careful with the club's aircraft as with their own. And most clubs have a wider range of risk exposure with aircraft of all types and complexity. In addition, flying clubs with aircraft used for training need more insurance than if membership is comprised of 5,000-hour pilots. Many who decide to form a flying club start by talking with aviation insurance brokers to make sure they can get the best rates while keeping risks to a minimum.

Flying Club Agreement

The agreement (sometimes called the constitution) establishing the flying club must cover a variety of legal topics to a level not required for co-ownerships and partnerships. More planes, more pilots, more misunderstandings, more to go wrong. The flying club agreement outlines how the club is formed and for what purpose, where it will get its assets (aircraft, etc.), how it will calculate and distribute expenses, the requirements for membership including costs, a job description for officers, and rules on how aircraft time will be managed and planes maintained.

A flying club typically is incorporated as a non-profit corporation, often as a 501(c)(7), a social or recreational club. The number refers to the IRS Code that explains their function as "organized for pleasure, recreation, and other nonprofitable purposes." They are simpler to manage than a 501(c)(3) that covers charitable and religious groups. Make sure you understand the differences and follow your attorney's recommendation when organizing your flying club.

Flying Club Bylaws

The flying group is formed and held together by bylaws, a legal document that outlines the terms of organization, membership, and operations including membership requirements, new member checkout, flight instructor requirements, unimproved airport operations, and insurance requirements. The bylaws will also cover dues, costs, and payments including fuel and oil purchases. Finally, the flying club bylaws will document how aircraft are scheduled and returned as the club's agreement on handling aircraft damage and repairs. There will be more legalese about governing law and arbitration just to cover any future problems.

In addition, members will probably be required to sign a rental agreement each time they use a club aircraft. This document will be much shorter and will review requirements, costs, and penalties.

Sadly, there aren't as many active flying clubs today as there were three decades ago. However, new ones are still being formed, especially around specific interests: light-sport aircraft, high-performance aircraft, warbirds, and other specialized flying that require many owners to keep the costs down. As you plan and organize your flying club, focus on clarifying its purpose and keep its mission statement as your guide through years of successful growth and flying.

Joining Other Frugal Pilots

Frugal pilots aren't cheap nor unsafe. Their buying and flying decisions are based on getting the greatest VALUE for each aviation dollar spent, not on squeezing every dollar until Lincoln yelps.

Frugal pilots aren't poor. They may or may not be financially rich, but they do know the significance of money and that a dollar saved wisely can be a dollar spent on more avgas or iPhones or retirement.

Frugal pilots aren't alone. There are many thousands of us who fly comfortably within a budget for a variety of good reasons: to go somewhere, to go nowhere, to see the world from above, to discover ourselves, to share recreation, to overcome fears, and/or to build an aviation career. At my airport, I hear many stories from grinning pilots who started out mowing lawns, washing airplanes, or taking on a second job to afford flying lessons. Over the years, these veteran pilots have logged thousands of hours in their owned or co-owned aircraft by being frugal – and safe.

Frugal Secrets

What are their secrets? No secrets, just seeking VALUE for each dollar traded for aviation. They rent, buy, or share their wings based on smart economic decisions made after clearly understanding WHY they fly. They keep it simple, manage their wants vs. needs, participate in aircraft maintenance, learn from their own experiences, learn from smarter pilots, shop smart, barter when they can, and combine purposes for each flight.

Some frugal pilots decide that their best option is to rent their wings as needed. For many, it's the right move – especially if they find an FBO with affordable, well-maintained aircraft nearby. They may find one or two favorite planes, purchase renter's insurance, and work a deal with the owner to prepay – or even barter services – for flight time.

Frugal pilots also consider sharing their wings to get the greatest value from their aviation budget. Few recreational pilots fly as many hours as they plan to when first getting into general aviation. The initial goal of maybe ten hours a month, often erodes to just a couple hours a month. Meanwhile, their plane sits alone in a hangar or at a tie-down awaiting the next annual inspection. The pilot is off with other activities until the next biennial flight review. Meantime, the fixed operating costs keep adding up and spouses question why.

Sharing Flying Costs

Eventually, it occurs to frugal pilots to consider sharing their wings with other frugal pilots. They determine that they can fly more and for less money if they share the fixed costs, operating costs, and reserves with other like-minded aviators. They may establish a co-ownership with two or three other pilots who all have their names on an aircraft registration. Or they find three to five members and go in for a more complex partnership to share a more complex aircraft. Or they start or join a flying club with a wider variety of airplanes and pilots with which to share. Each structure has its own advantages and disadvantages to fit the needs of most frugal pilots.

Share Your Frugality

That's a summary of how and why frugal pilots fly on a budget. There are many variations on these ideas with dozens of examples of each.

So it's YOUR turn! Please take a few minutes to share your experiences, suggestions, and tips on being a Frugal Pilot so that I may share them with readers of this column. Why do you fly? How many hours do you fly each year? What type of flying do you do? How do you keep down the costs of going up? How do you participate in your aircraft's maintenance, if at all? What are your experiences, good and bad, with sharing your wings?

You can email me at Dan@FrugalPilot.com with your own tips for frugal pilots. Flying is a community and your experiences can be helpful to other frugal flyers.

Frugal Pilots Share Tips

"You're a pilot? You must be rich!" Isn't that the impression that many folks have about pilots?

In reality, owner-pilots typically are no richer than those who own a boat or an RV. Many a boat or motor home gets less use annually than our aircraft. And wouldn't the roads and waterways be safer if trailer-towers and motor-boaters got the level of training that pilots got?

Of course, frugal pilots aren't poor. They can afford one of life's greatest toys. The main point of being frugal about flying is that you get more from every aviation dollar spent.

In my last column, I asked for your ways of keeping down the costs of going up, your frugal pilot tips. Here are a few.

Kyle Ludwick of Indianapolis offered a wide variety of frugal pilot tips. First, start out at a small local airport training with a Part 61 (independent) flight school where costs typically are lower. "Yes, students can get certificates faster under Part 141 (FAA-certified schools) with less hours, but it's definitely not a frugal way to go..." unless you want an aviation career. Kyle later went pro with a degree in Aviation Business Administration and multiple commercial certificates at a Part 141 school – then went on to work for the school. His recreational flying started in a classic

Piper Apache owned by a partnership. Now he's in a flying club through his job and flies their Cessna 172s for about half the cost of owning it outright.

Making a living at flying is a common frugal tip. Kyle Cameron of Whitehorse, Yukon Territory got his AME (Aircraft Maintenance Engineer) licence (similar to the FAA's Airframe and Powerplant certificate) "so I could do my own maintenance." Smart!

Humberto Villalobos of Toronto also went professional to fund his flying. His advice: "Become a flight instructor. If you want to learn something, teach it." He teaches both flight and ground school, recently retiring from his factory job to fly. "I fly about 200 hours a year and love it. I even get paid to do it."

Chris Strube of Lillooet, British Columbia, is a piano tuner and repairman. How does he afford flying? "I use my plane for business as well as pleasure. This has three benefits: It allows a tax deduction, it lowers hourly costs because I use the plane much more (100-150 hours a year), and it keeps me current and (I hope) sharp." Chris flies a classic 1965 Mooney M20E with fuel injection. More tips? Chris refills his own oxygen system, filling an aviation cylinder from a larger medical cylinder. And he does all the aircraft maintenance he is legally allowed to do, such as oil changes, plug cleaning, brake pads, etc., using mechanics that allow owner-assisted annuals and repairs. It not only saves Chris money, it helps him better understand his flying machine.

Frank Schilchting of Grand Forks, British Columbia, is a trucker by trade. How does he fly frugally? "An ultralight is the key to affordable aviation. My plane cost is $25 an hour to fly. It only burns 15 liters (4 gallons) of car gas an hour. Why buy a four-place aircraft? How often will you be flying with four people? I cruise at 80 miles an hour. Why go fast? You just miss all of the awesome scenery."

One more frugal pilot to hear from: me. I pay for my flying as a part-time contractor serving as a small community airport manager. I help the municipal owner keep up on the FAA requirements and grant applications, test the fuel, help manage hangars and tie downs, and promote the airport. Not hard work, but very enjoyable. It funds my flying.

Frugal Pilots Offer More Tips

One of the best ways to fly more while spending less is shopping smart. Frugal pilots know this. But they don't all realize how creative shopping smart can become.

Shopping Smart

Reader Dennis Martin of Menominee, Michigan is a creative frugal pilot. He reports "I recently overhauled the Lycoming O-360 in my Cessna 170B. It turned out that almost every part on the engine is PMA'd (FAA Parts Manufacturer Approval) by multiple sources, which really helps drive the costs down. Buying everything at one time from one source saved big on shipping. There is so much competition on things like cylinders that you can get BRAND NEW cylinder kits for about the same cost as overhauling/overboring. Also, it turns out that a cam kit with lifters and tappets was cheaper than buying the parts individually." Buy a popular airplane and shop smart for parts.

Dennis admits that he is an A&P (airframe and powerplant) mechanic. "But even if I wasn't, the disassembly and reassembly goes quick. The tedious (expensive) part is all the cleanup, parts wrangling, shipping, etc. – and you don't need to be an A&P or even particularly handy to do that." Dennis notes that you can inspect your own magnetos and save hundreds of dollars using the manuals available online as well as calling the manufacturer's technical support. His second tip is to do as much of the work as you can yourself – A&P or not.

How much did frugal Dennis save? "I got a complete overhaul for a little over $10,000. That same engine sent out to a shop would be closer to $20,000." One of the reasons for the higher price is that many FBO shops today crate the engine up and ship it out to a remanufacturer – one more step in an expensive process. And the difference in price will buy many tanksful of avgas.

Reducing Taxes

Another way to reduce flying costs is to pay less taxes. I am not advocating hiding your aircraft to avoid taxes – after all, some of the states and cities actually improve aviation with the money they collect from various taxes on aviation. Some do not. However, many government entities offer smart aircraft owners opportunities to legitimately reduce or eliminate their tax expense.

For example, in California and some other states, you can report your older (35+ year old) plane as an "Aircraft of Historical Importance." If eligible, city or county personal property tax may be waved – if you comply with their requirements. That sometimes means that you show your aircraft at public events through the year, but that is just one more good excuse to go flying. As you can imagine, the local assessor's office isn't going to call up all area pilots to offer this exemption, so you're going to have to do some calling to see what is available. You may find that your state leaves aircraft tax assessment to the county and they choose not to do it. Hangaring your aircraft at one airport may offer tax savings over another just a few miles away. You won't know if you don't ask. Your local or regional pilot's association may already have done this homework.

Another example of reducing tax costs is to speak with a tax attorney as you buy or sell an aircraft. Many states require that you pay sales tax on the transaction value. The five states that currently don't add sales tax to a purchase are Alaska, Delaware, Montana, New Hampshire, and Oregon. Others tax some purchases and not others. It can pay to find out.

Private and commercial aircraft sales may be treated differently in your state or municipality. Leases often have different taxation regulations than buying your wings. The National Business Aviation Association (NBAA.org) offers a free white paper on State Aviation Tax. Knowing how the sales or user tax system works where you live can save you many thousands of dollars as you purchase your next plane.

One more idea: Fuel tax paid may be an allowable deduction on your federal or state taxes. Again, talk with a tax expert – especially one who is a pilot.

Need some more info? Visit http://www.aopa.org/Pilot-Resources/Aircraft-Ownership/The-Pilots-Guide-to-Taxes. It offers helpful facts on income tax, sales and use tax, and personal property tax as they relate to aircraft.

Frugal Pilots Kiss

It is great to be a part of the general aviation community where pilots share their ideas to help each other with knowledge and kindness. I especially like to see the many helpful frugal tips offered online from readers of my column. They add their own proven experiences that helped them fly more while spending less. For example, many readers have responded with information on their own tax laws after last month's tip on "Reducing Taxes." Thanks to everyone who has contributed.

I recently received a slew of great tips from Patrick Piper of Houston, Texas. Patrick has been flying for nearly 40 years, everything from a 1946 Stinson to his current bird, a 1964D Cessna 150 that he bought as a basket case and rebuilt back to flying condition. Patrick did what some frugal pilots do: he earned an A&P license to reduce his costs and learn more about his aircraft than the typical owner knows. That makes sense for some frugal pilots, but not for others. To get an A&P license you need to attend an FAA-approved aviation maintenance technical school, get up to 30 months of experience and pass some written, oral, and practical tests. Others who want to be mechanics on their own plane opt to build an experimental aircraft. Still others simply read a lot about aircraft maintenance and help their friendly mechanic with owner-assisted maintenance.

Here are some of Patrick's recommendations and my extensions, many of them mentioned in prior columns of The Frugal Pilot:

- Keep up with avgas fuel prices in your area as there can be as much as $1 a gallon difference during the current volatile fuel market. Check AirNav.com, 100LL.com, and iPad apps like ForeFlight.

- Fly at 55-65% power unless you're in a hurry...and most frugal pilots aren't. You can save 10-20% on fuel costs.

- Find a less-expensive hangar at a nearby airport. Not always an option, but worth checking into. Otherwise, ask your airport for a discount for paying hangar rents annually. Some offer a 10% discount if they don't have to bill you every month.

- Consider a tiedown instead of a hangar. Many aircraft do just fine outside in temperate climates and you can save $100 or more each month by renting a tiedown – enough to pay for a basic annual inspection.

- Don't get more aircraft than you can afford. It's the Frugal Pilot's mantra. If recreational flying typically means just you and maybe one friend or relative, opt for a two-seat aircraft rather than four or more. Fuel typically is half, maintenance is less, insurance is less, and your little aircraft can fly anywhere the larger ones can.

- If you're considering a light-sport aircraft (LSA) for medical reasons (requires a driver's license rather than a third-class medical), opt for a classic LSA, an older aircraft that meets LSA requirements. New LSAs typically are over $100,000. For more info, visit SportFlyingGuide.com or SportFlying.aero.

- Don't be shy about asking for gas money. A two-seat GA aircraft burns about $30 an hour in fuel and a four-seater about double of that. You can't legally charge a specific fee to passengers unless you have a commercial certificate and the aircraft meets other criteria, but the FAA is okay with sharing operating expenses between the pilot and passengers. Operating expenses include both fixed costs (hangar, insurance, etc.) and variable per-hour costs (fuel, maintenance). A frugal pilot knows how much per it costs to fly the aircraft. Simply split it equally. It's much easier if you're splitting the costs of a rental aircraft, wet.

- Find tax-deductible opportunities. If you own a business, how can you use your aircraft in it to expense some of the costs. If you're an employee, will your employer pay shared operating expenses for your flying him or her to a business destination? If you are doing flights for charity, keep good records and use them for tax-deductible donations. For all tax opportunities, keep good records.

- Review your insurance each year. Report your flying hours to the insurance company as your experience may qualify you for a lower rate. Recheck your hull insurance. Do you really need that much to replace your plane? Or more? Shop around among aviation insurance brokers. Every dollar you save on insurance can go toward more avgas.

One of the most important frugal pilot tips this column points out is that I don't know everything about flying on a budget. You may not either. We all rely on the experience and help of other like-minded pilots to find ways of keeping down the costs of going up. Talk with other pilots, asking them how they manage the expenses of general aviation.

Frugal pilots Keep It Safe and Simple...KISS.

Frugal Pilots Dream of Full Owner Maintenance

Imagine owning a frugal aircraft – a Cessna 120 through 172, Piper Cub and PA-11 through 28, Aeronca, Taylorcraft, and even some Grummans and Beeches – and being able to work on them legally. Yes, even sign them off for the annual inspection. Just imagine.

Hard to imagine? Then go to Canada! Canadian aircraft owners can perform maintenance and sign off on a wide variety of recreational aircraft maintenance and repair. It's all spelled out in Canadian Aviation Regulations' Part V – Standard 507 – Owner Maintenance. In addition, the Canadian Owners and Pilots Association (COPAnational.org) offers a guide on the Owner Maintenance Category, what owners can and cannot do, and eligibility requirements.

The Owner-Maintenance category, says COPA, was developed to allow certain older certified fixed-wing airplanes and gliders to be maintained and restored under similar regulations as amateur-built aircraft. OM aircraft are pretty well limited to daytime VFR, but their pilots can have a lot of fun before the sun sets.

What work can aircraft owners do on O-M category aircraft? They can maintain the aircraft, conduct and sign for the annual inspection, refurbish or overhaul all or part of the plane, install certified and uncertified parts, install or replace any instruments or avionics, modify an airplane (within certain limits), rebuild an aircraft that is out of service, and sign the maintenance release.

And guess what? The owner can hire someone to do some or all of the work on the eligible aircraft – an Aircraft Maintenance Engineer (AME), an amateur builder or Uncle Harry. After final inspection, the AME or owner/pilot can sign the maintenance release and it's time to go flying.

There are about 400 eligible aircraft models in the Canadian OM category, everything from an Aero Commander 100 to a Wolf Hirth Doppelraab IV. If the list isn't long enough to fit your wings, you can add it to the list following CAR Standard 507.03(6)(e). Basically, eligible aircraft weren't built to carry more than four people, weigh less than 4,000 pounds (1,814 kg), are powered by a single normally-aspirated piston engine, are not considered a commercial aircraft and the type and model hasn't been manufactured during the last five years.

The process for converting an eligible Canadian aircraft from certified category to Owner Maintenance category is relatively simple, easier than getting a U.S. homebuilt aircraft certified as experimental. Fill out some forms, pay a $250 fee, and post a "Special Certificate of Airworthiness: Owner Maintenance" in the cockpit.

Wow! How do American frugal pilots sign up? Hold on, Socko, let's hear...the rest of the story.

Canada's OM Category has been around for about 20 years. However, by 2013, just 4 percent of all Canadian aircraft were registered in the OM category. Ouch! Why so few? Well, in Canada, selling an OM aircraft is about as tough as selling a U.S.

experimental aircraft – and for some of the same reasons. The owner, not a licensed mechanic, can perform all repairs and sign off on airworthiness. Now we all know that an experimental aircraft is probably better maintained than many certified aircraft. That's because the owner is flying it, not some mechanic who may or may not even have a pilot license. But the perception to many is that A&P-inspected aircraft are safer than owner-maintained aircraft. True in many cases, false in others, but that is a popular perception.

However, the largest reason why the Canadian OM category isn't more popular is the U.S. Federal Aviation Administration. Since 2002, the FAA bans Canadian OM category aircraft from being sold – or even flying – in the U.S. With so much free trade going on every day between these two friendly countries, many Canadian pilots just don't want to limit the market to selling their aircraft just to Canadians.

Okay. How about converting an OM aircraft back to certified in Canada or the U.S.? Not so easy. The original airworthiness certificate that the plane came out of the factory with is no longer valid. The engine, propeller and all life-limited parts on the aircraft were permanently etched with an "X". For example, the Cessna 140 was legally made a Cessna 140X. And you can bet that every inch of the OM aircraft must be overhauled by an A&P mechanic and signed off before the new certificate is issued. Big Canadian bucks! The OM category was designed to be one-way.

Of course, there's much more to this story. However, it is relatively clear that even if the FAA someday decides to let Canadian OM aircraft fly in U.S. airspace – such as to Oshkosh, for example – the chances of the FAA establishing a similar Owner Maintenance category for us frugal pilots in the U.S. are slim to none. Consider how long it took ultralight and light-sport aircraft rules to be established. And don't forget the ongoing third-class medical battle. So, for now, U.S. frugal pilots must imagine.

Frugal Pilots Vs. Aircraft Mechanics

My article on aircraft maintenance that can be performed by the owner in Canada but not the U.S., stirred up a lively discussion among readers. Reader Greg W. summarized it best, noting that the owner of a U.S. standard category aircraft can maintain the aircraft, refurbish or overhaul all or part of the plane, install certified parts, install or replace many instruments or avionics, modify the aircraft (within limits), and even rebuild an aircraft out of service – as long as it is under the supervision and signed off by an FAA-licensed A&P/IA mechanic. "Finding a mechanic to work with you may take time, especially if you want to do a lot of changes. Give the mechanic time to trust your abilities and you will be amazed at what an owner can do."

The chances of the FAA changing the rules on owner maintenance anytime soon are slim. Meantime, we frugal pilots can continue the search for qualified aviation mechanics who will assist us in performing maintenance on our aircraft at our competence level. Even better, we can find mechanics who are willing to teach us to improve our mechanical competence and understanding.

But let me play the devil's advocate for a moment. As much as many aviation mechanics love aircraft, it is still a job. They must pay the rent, pay taxes, buy tools, pay for insurance, keep up on all the FAA rule changes and requirements, and maybe make enough to go flying once in a while. Oh yeah, and food. You can see why some mechanics see owner-assisted maintenance as cutting into their livelihood. Imagine your car mechanic letting you help with a brake job or an engine rebuild. It often is through their love of aviation that these mechanics allow owners to assist with the annual inspection and common repairs. In most cases, it is faster – and more profitable – for them to perform the maintenance and repairs themselves rather than supervising another, then signing off that the aircraft is airworthy.

As a reminder, a frugal pilot isn't cheap. We're not looking for the cheapest parts and labor. We're looking for value. We want to understand our aircraft better, but we're not ready to buy all our parts at Walmart and install them as best we can. We are drivers in the third dimension: pilots! We need an additional level of safety over two-dimensional car drivers. Our vehicles are more complex, they move faster, and they go places even cellphone signals don't. So it is smart for us frugal pilots who own their aircraft to seek out mechanics who are highly qualified to assist us in owner maintenance while they still make a living. There are many places in the flying budget where we can save money without being cheap.

So I suggest that if you wish to perform more of your aircraft's maintenance and repairs that you do so looking for value. Start by finding a qualified mechanic who will help you determine what you can safely do to your aircraft and what you should not. Don't expect to save much money at first as training is as expensive as doing. And your mechanic needs to make a living, too.

Where to start? Ask among your pilot friends. One pilot I know found his mechanic 300 miles away, which is just two hours in his aircraft. By doing a pre-inspection inspection at his home airport he can perform many of the basic maintenance steps without leaving home. Anything that requires a mechanic's sign-off is done with his friendly mechanic. Did I mention that the mechanic's airport is near a golf resort?

You can start closer to home, but you're not limited to your home airport. Seek out a mechanic who will work with you – and maybe even train you. Expand your comfort zone, but know your limits. If you don't do oil changes on your own car, you may not want to do them on your aircraft. Let your car teach you a few things about working on a vehicle including what tools and knowledge you need. Of course, cars and planes aren't the same (they both have their own Disney movie!), but they are sufficiently similar to help you build mechanical skills on your car before applying them to your aircraft.

U.S. owner-pilots can work within the FAA system, rather than just complain about it, to keep our aircraft both safe and cost-effective. That's what being a frugal pilot is all about.

Frugal Pilots Join the Club

One of my 10 Tips for Frugal Pilots is "Learn from smarter pilots." No matter what you fly or where, there's someone nearby who knows more about aviation than you do. Unsolicited advice can be annoying, but finding smart pilots who can teach without lecturing is an opportunity to improve your skills — and lower your flying costs — without having to depend on just your experiences and your pocketbook. As you identify these smart and helpful pilots, cultivate their friendships and save yourself a ton of money. I especially recommended membership in aviation organizations that fit your needs: the Aircraft Owners and Pilots Association, the Experimental Aircraft Association, etc.

Let me expand on that concept and suggest that you seriously consider joining or adding a "type club" to your knowledge base. Typically, for a dues payment of less than an hour of avgas each year you can add the wisdom of hundreds of pilots with common goals and unique prospectives.

First, let's start with an inventory. Here are the 20 most-popular aircraft models that have been built for the North American general aviation market in the past century, by the (approximate) production numbers:

➢ Cessna 172 Skyhawk (43,000)

- ➤ Piper PA-28 Cherokee (33,000)
- ➤ Cessna 150/152 (31,000)
- ➤ Cessna 182 Skylane (23,000)
- ➤ Piper J-3 Cub (20,000)
- ➤ Beechcraft Bonanza (17,000)
- ➤ Chotia Weedhopper (13,000)
- ➤ Piper Pacer (10,000)
- ➤ Aeronca Champion (10,000)
- ➤ Cessna 210 Centurion (9,000)
- ➤ Piper PA-18 Super Cub (9,000)
- ➤ Beechcraft 18 "Twin Beech" (9,000)
- ➤ Boeing-Stearman 75 (8,000)
- ➤ Cessna 206 (8,000)
- ➤ Piper PA-32 (8,000)
- ➤ Cessna 120/140 (7,000)
- ➤ Piper PA-23 (7,000)
- ➤ Cessna 310 (6,000)
- ➤ Cessna 180 (6,000)
- ➤ Stinson 108 (5,000)

Few surprises here (except for the Chotia Weedhopper, the only ultralight on the list). Cessna is the most popular brand with about 133,000 GA aircraft on this list. Piper follows with about 87,000. And, of course, the list doesn't include experimental/homebuilt aircraft brands or the light-sport aircraft category that started just a decade ago.

My point is that in addition to membership in the AOPA and/or EAA, frugal pilots should join at least one type club to get specific advice and resources from "smarter pilots." For example, the Cessna 150/152 Club (cessna150152.com) has approximately 1,000 owner/pilots who fly and maintain these classic trainers. The club forum is active on topics from modifications and STCs to information on their annual fly-in. Members also can access 25+ years of club newsletters on all topics imaginable plus a database of 150/152 aircraft photos by N-number. It also includes travelogues by pilots who have flown in specific regions, cross-country, or to destinations such as Oshkosh or Sun N Fun. Online club dues are just $35 a year ($50 for a postal subscription).

Other GA type clubs work similarly: smart owners and pilots with tons of knowledge (and opinions) share with others. Here are some resources:

➢ Aeronca Aviators (aeronca.org)

➢ American Bonanza Society (bonanza.org)

➢ Beechcraft (beachaeroclub.org)

➢ Cessna 172 Club (cessna172club.com)

➢ Cessna Flyer Association (cessnaflyer.org)

➢ Cessna Owner Organization (cessnaowner.org)

➢ Cessna Pilots Association (cessna.org)

➢ International 180-185 Club (skywagons.org)

➢ International Cessna 195 Club (cessna195.org)

➢ International Stinson Club (stinsonclub.org)

➢ Luscombe (luscombeassoc.org)

➢ Piper Owner Society (piperowner.org)

- ➤ Short Wing Piper Club (shortwingpiperclub.org)

- ➤ Stearman (stearman.net)

- ➤ The Piper Cub Club (cubclub.org)

- ➤ The Skylark Association (cessna175.org)

- ➤ Van's Aircraft Club (vansairforce.net)

- • Vintage Piper Aircraft Club (vintagepiper.com)

- • Weedhopper (ulav8r.com)

And the list goes on. There are aviation clubs and online forums for canard aircraft builders (canardzone.com), vintage ultralights and light planes (vula.org), Zenith builders and flyers (zenith.aero), plus the Vintage Aircraft Association (eaavintage.org) and Warbirds of America (warbirds-eaa.org), both divisions of the EAA.

If you can't find an aviation type club or interest club to fit your wings, you're just not trying hard enough. There are dozens. And if you still can't find one, start one. Chances are there are others out there who are smart pilots looking for friendly skies. You can start with an online search at http://registry.faa.gov/aircraftinquiry/, entering a make and model number for results by state, then by owner. For example, there are nearly 1,000 Beech Model 19 or 23 (Musketeers) in the FAA Registry. Make sure you search for the manufacturer's model number (19 or 23) rather than the marketing name (Musketeer).

Your Frugal Flight Mission

Professional pilots have flight missions. A commercial pilot's flight mission is to safely fly a specific aircraft with an identified weight to an explicit destination on schedule. Law enforcement pilots perform missions that involve highway surveillance and speed monitoring. NASA has specific flight missions and procedures to make sure their expensive flights have a purpose and expected outcome.

Private pilots also have flight missions, though their goals and descriptions are less formal. Even so, all flights should have a mission – especially those by frugal pilots who are looking for the greatest value for each aviation dollar spent. These flight missions don't have to include specific waypoints, but should include defined objectives. Here are common reasons why frugal pilots fly:

Destination flying. Frugal pilots often define their flying by *where* they fly, such as to specific airports, new airports, for business, for scenery, or for a great restaurant. They may also define where they go by how they go: fast or slow. Many pilots prefer one over the other.

Home flying. Many pilots would rather stay in a small geographic area, simply flying the pattern to someday achieve the ultimate goal of the perfect landing. Or they have a specific course they most enjoy flying, taking in the scenery and landmarks, but typically only landing at their home airport.

Prospective adjustment. Many pilots fly because it literally adds a new dimension to their lives. Looking down from 3,000 feet, weeds are invisible. Flying your wings in familiar surroundings can be a real stress-reducer at the beginning or end of a workday or week.

Self-discovery. Pilots have other titles: father, mother, husband, wife, partner, parent, employer, employee, professional, friend, etc. But they all are secondary to *pilot-in-command*. In the left seat, they are in control. All the hard work and study that brought them to this title and position gives them individual pride found in few other personal endeavors.

Sharing. Many pilots prefer not to fly alone. The fuel costs about the same no matter whether the flight is solo or with a passenger or two. So why not share the ride. Maybe it's a colleague from work, a spouse, a child or grandchild, or someone who told you they'd love to go flying someday soon. Flying is a gift to be shared.

Challenge. Not everyone feels totally comfortable in an airplane high above the ground – including many pilots. In fact, that's why some became pilots, to overcome a natural fear with the irrefutable facts of aeronautics. Once accomplished, they help others overcome similar fears. They fly for the challenge of learning and applying the rules of aviation.

Professional opportunities. Many pilots fly for a living. Their private pilot or sport pilot certificate is just the first of many. It's a worthwhile goal that motivates them to select an aircraft and fund their flying, typically on a budget, to meet specific professional goals.

Those are common missions for many frugal pilots. Most flights will include more than one mission, such as the sharing of destination flying. The important point for frugal pilots is to know why, when and how you fly, then match your needs and wants to your wallet. Logging and review your flight missions can help you get more from your flying dollars.

For example, after reviewing his log book for the past year a frugal pilot may realize that he flew a four-seater solo 90 percent of the time, primarily within an hour of the home airport. A mission review will help him decide whether his airplane is the most appropriate for his flying. Maybe a two-seater is a smarter choice. Or renting an aircraft would be a better budgetary move. A key to frugal flying is knowing why you fly and to make sure that your equipment, investments and expenses efficiently support that key element.

In other cases, mission reviews help pilots determine that they really need – or maybe don't need – an IFR aircraft and rating. Or that they would utilize a higher-performance aircraft if they could share it with partners. Or that they are ready to start making money flying as a CFI.

Your mission, should you choose to accept it, is to get the greatest value you can from every dollar you spend as a frugal pilot.

Rethinking Your Frugal Wings

The purpose of summarizing why you fly is to help you decide <u>what</u> you should fly. Are you flying an aircraft that is more than you need for what you want to do? Put another way, are you paying for things you don't really use?

No matter why and what you fly, this is a good thing to review every few years as maybe your flying goals have changed or your flying budget needs some adjustment to get the most from every aviation dollar you spend. Frugal flying isn't about being cheap; it's about getting the greatest value.

So you've reviewed your logbooks and decided which of the common flight missions you've spent the most time completing – and had the most fun with. They include destination flying, home flying, prospective adjustment, self-discovery, sharing, challenge, and professional opportunities. Most private pilots focus their flying on one or two of these missions. A wings review can help you decide whether what you fly closely matches why you fly.

Periodically, aviation magazines run a series of articles on common aircraft, listing the top dozen most popular models, what they cost, how they fly, and how to buy them. Some are simple two-seaters while others are more popular four-seat and larger models designed for long-distance flying missions. All of us read those articles to determine if there isn't something better out there to match our current flight missions. That's smart.

What often isn't covered is how to select from the hundreds or maybe thousands of specific aircraft available at any given time. How should you select one Piper Tri-Pacer over another, for example? That decision probably will impact your flying budget more than choosing one model over another.

To choose between specific aircraft, first review your budget against your comfort level of working on your aircraft. As a licensed mechanic, you may choose a basket-case aircraft while a pilot friend who doesn't do his own oil changes may prefer something ready to fly. The difference in purchase price can be dramatic with a DIY aircraft priced at half the cost of one that doesn't need anything, mechanical or cosmetic. Here are some suggestions as you choose one specific aircraft over another:

Engine: At least half the price of a used simple aircraft is for the engine. Know how much an engine replacement will cost on your selected model. Get costs on a major overhaul and estimate how much time is left in the one you're considering. Also review your log book. If you calculate that the engine probably has at least 500 hours more until overhaul, how long will it take you to fly 500 hours? Five years? Ten? Will you keep the plane that long?

Systems: Are there any system problems that will now or may soon ground your aircraft? Replacing an instrument or repairing brakes are minor system problems that can be resolved less expensively than extensive airframe corrosion. You may decide to tackle a DIY aircraft with corrosion problems – if you know about them before you buy. That's where a pre-purchase inspection by a trusted mechanic can pay for itself.

Cosmetics: Painting an aircraft isn't cheap, but it isn't required to make it airworthy. Ugly Ducks fly as far as Swans. If your flying budget must choose between an iPad and wheel fairings, go for the one that makes flying more fun.

Log books: Historical engine and airframe log books aren't required to fly your aircraft, just the current ones. However, they are invaluable to your decision whether to purchase an aircraft and for how much. They tell you not only what has been done to the aircraft over the years, but also indicate how meticulous the owner and mechanics have been. And they can help you estimate how many hours a year it has been flown. Sloppy records may indicate sloppy work. At best, incomplete or poorly kept log books make it more difficult for you to estimate the cost of future maintenance and repairs.

Location: Not as important in selecting an aircraft as other considerations, its location can make a difference. Not only is a nearby aircraft easier to inspect, it also can indicate where and how it has been flown. Also, it is easier to perform research on the aircraft by interviewing people at the airport where the plane was based. And it will be less expensive for your favorite mechanic to perform a pre-purchase inspection. Finally, the cost of flying an aircraft cross-country after purchase can add a few hundred to a few thousand dollars to the price.

These are all important considerations as you select one specific aircraft over another in your search for your frugal plane.

Tips for Frugal Renters

Not all pilots fly their owned wings. For a variety of reasons, many frugal pilots choose to rent aircraft. They may not fly enough hours to justify owning. They may own a simple aircraft but sometimes rent specialized planes for more capacity, IFR flights, or to add new types to their log book.

There is no specific point at which frugal pilots should consider getting rid of their plane for lack of use and renting. Many say that for flying fewer than 50 hours a year, renting is cheaper. For others, the number is higher or lower. And there are more reasons than frugality to consider renting aircraft. Most of the tips for frugal pilots apply to those who rent their wings. In addition, frugal renters have a few more decisions to make. Here are some tips for frugal aircraft renters.

Know why you fly

A couple of articles ago, we discussed annually reviewing your flying mission by asking "Why do I fly?" and assessing your logbooks to confirm or deny your assumption. At that point, many pilots reconsider owning an airplane and think about renting – or maybe owning one type and periodically renting another type. In any case, it is important to periodically review the reality of your flying. Maybe renting is your best option.

Know your budget

Even if flying missions don't change over the years, budgets often do. Instead of flying 125 hours a year, you're now flying 25 for one of a variety of reasons. Jobs, families, responsibilities, personal goals, and time available for flying are upsized or downsized by life. Review and adjust your current flying budget annually. Maybe you should be renting your aircraft – or maybe buying one instead of renting.

Make it easier

Renting an aircraft can be a hassle, requiring a check ride, document review, reserving a plane when you need it, and preflighting an aircraft you may not be familiar with. You can make some of these steps easier by selecting your primary rental service and working out the trust issues before your first rental flight. Get the check ride out of the way, select two or three preferred aircraft from the hangar, and make sure the rental service has an easy way to reserve aircraft by phone or online, and get your credit card information into their secure database.

Many frugal pilots are signing up with aircraft rental networks such as OpenAirplane.com that standardize pre-rental requirements to make renting easier nationwide. Once you are accepted in the system, your certification, logbook, and financial information are available to member FBO rental services with a Universal Pilot Checkout. You may not need a check flight if you are renting aircraft that you have prior experience with.

You also can make renting easier on your wallet by purchasing blocks of rental time in advance of use. Many FBOs offer a ten percent discount for prepaid rental fees. That's like getting one free flying hour for every ten.

Get renters insurance

FBOs that rent aircraft protect their aircraft assets with commercial aircraft insurance. If the plane crashes, they get another one. But what about you and your passengers? Most aircraft rental agreements don't adequately cover you. Just how much renters insurance you need depends on what the FBO covers, but most renter policies are set up to fill the gaps.

When purchasing an aircraft renters insurance policy, the rate will depend on the depth of your logbook, what you plan to fly, and from where. Additional charges are applied if you rent multi-engine aircraft or are flying in Alaska or Hawaii. If you have had an aircraft insurance policy in the past, contact their agent first as you may get a preferred customer discount.

Aircraft renters insurance is also called non-owned insurance and is for pilots who fly other people's aircraft. For example, if you are a member of a flying club or often fly aircraft you don't own, seriously consider non-owned insurance. Even if you do own a plane, your current policy may or may not cover you in someone else's airplane. Find out before it becomes an issue.

Preflight your rental

One of the disadvantages of flying rental aircraft is that you don't know who flew it last. The pilot may have been ex-military with an extensive preflight inspection – or a kick-the-tires-and-light-the-fire pilot. Just in case your chosen rental aircraft doesn't have a checklist, consider buying a CheckMate, QREF, or other laminated model-specific checklist for your flight bag.

Flying is a safe and enjoyable pastime, even if you're renting your wings. By being a frugal pilot, you can fly more and spend less.

Frugal Pilots On Part 23 Reorganization

Frugal pilots and others heavily lobbied their representatives on H.R. 1848, the Small Airplane Revitalization Act and it passed unanimously – 411 to 0 – on July 18, 2013. A similar bill soon was passed by the U.S. Senate (S. 1072) and was signed by the President that November.

The legislation recognized that since 2003, the U.S. lost an average of 10,000 active private pilots a year, partially due to a lack of cost-effective, new small aircraft. The Great LSA Hope of 2004 was that light-sport aircraft and the new sport pilot certificate would revitalize the recreational end of general aviation. Didn't happen. New aircraft were well above $100,000 and new pilot rules didn't really solve the problem of making flying more affordable.

The 2013 legislation directed the Federal Aviation Administration to issue a final rule that reorganized part 23 of title 14, Code of Federal Regulations. That's the part that covers airworthiness standards for normal, utility, aerobatic, and commuter aircraft. The FAA was given until December 15, 2015 – two years – to come up with revised rules.

How's it going?

Not so well. A year after the 2013 bill passed, an FAA spokesperson told Congress that it would miss the 2015 deadline by two years, 2017, even though the FAA said it had been working on part 23 reform since 2008.

What's the hold up?

A representative of the Government Accountability Office (GAO) told subcommittee members in 2014 that the FAA is moving in the direction of reforming regulations but faces the slow and difficult task of changing its culture as part of that effort. The FAA concedes that change is needed, even overdue, but admits that it cannot do so within the legislated timeline – not even close.

The FAA says that reorganizing regulations isn't quite that simple. Major changes to part 23 also impact parts 91 (general operating and flight rules) and part 135 (commuter and on-demand operations). Staffing, they say, is short and prioritization of regulation reviews and changes is low.

Is that true?

The Federal Aviation Administration is responsible for the safety of civil (non-military) aviation in the U.S. Their annual budget of about $9 billion a year covers regulating everything from pilots to airplanes to airports to airspace. They are in charge of general aviation as well as commercial aviation.

The fact is that the FAA is a *bureaucracy*: a system of government in which most of the important decisions are made by officials rather than by elected representatives. Like all bureaucracies, it isn't omnipotent nor always efficient. And like all bureaucracies it is chock full of people who are really trying to do a good job in offices and cubicle farms with many others who don't really care.

Opinion Alert

In my opinion, it's the FAA's fault that part 23 reorganization will miss the mandated deadline, and maybe the next one. But it's ultimately Congress' fault. Each budget year, Congress reduces Department of Transportation (DOT) and FAA funding while adding more responsibilities and directives. Earlier this year, Congress extended FAA funding for another six months – yes, just six months. In 2011, it virtually shut the FAA down and immediately furloughed 4,000 employees – and idled 70,000 airport construction workers – by allowing their funding to expire. Who wants to work hard for an employer that acts like it is going out of business?

The Small Airplane Revitalization Act of 2013 is a good idea. Frugal pilots know this. They also know that FAA regulations are way too complex for recreational pilots (and small airport managers, let me tell you). Something needs to be done to apply safety rules and regulations appropriately based on actual risk. Something needs to be done to make the FAA more efficient and responsive. But first something needs to be done to make Congress smarter about money management. Direct it, fund it, manage it. That is what our chosen representatives are supposed to be doing.

A frugal pilot seeks good value from every dollar spent. We need a frugal Congress. Please ask your congressional representatives to fund the FAA long-term...then to hold the FAA accountable to responsively do its job.

Starting A Frugal Pilot Flying Club

The Wright Brothers Flying Club (motto: Wright side up!) was the first of thousands of organizations intended to enjoy flying on a budget. Though not as popular as they were in the 1970s, flying clubs are resurging in interest throughout the country – especially among budget-conscious pilots.

Previous articles covered flying clubs flying club basics and crafting a flying club agreement. Following is a different prospective: how to form a frugal flying club with a focus on one of the most complex expenses: insurance. Keeping an eye on insurance costs and opportunities as you form a club can help you make smarter and more cost-effective decisions.

How do I know this? Recently, Bill Sneed of Aviation Insurance Resources (AIR; air-pros.com) shared some valuable tips with me on forming a flying club with a focus on getting the best value. Bill has been a pilot since 1974 and flew as a California crop duster. He's worked for AVEMCO and Falcon/Great Lakes and was president of the AOPA Insurance Agency before joining AIR. He's a big advocate for flying clubs.

Flying clubs are about the passion pilots have for flight as well as their budgets. For many pilots, the cost of owning an aircraft is beyond individual means. Flying clubs offer a way for frugal pilots to co-own an aircraft. Bill offers sound advice on the three factors that all flying clubs need to consider: type of aircraft, number of pilots, and insurance coverage.

Choosing a plane

The least expensive and easiest to insure club planes are under 200 horsepower, fixed wing, fixed gear planes manufactured by Cessna, Piper, and Beach. Of course, many other GA aircraft can be and are insured in flying clubs, but the least expensive ones to insure are the ones that are the most popular.

Bill recommends starting a frugal flying club with four-seat Cessna 172s and Piper PA-28s for the lowest initial purchase and lowest operating and insuring expenses.

Choosing members

How many members should your frugal flying club have? For the lowest per-member cost, aim for less than ten member pilots per aircraft. Five-to-ten-per plane works out the most economical while allowing ample time for flying for each member pilot.

Old pilots? New pilots? Yes! Successful flying clubs have a broad mix of pilots, from students to veterans. Often, the enthusiasm of newer pilots rubs off on the more experienced ones who may not still be in love with flying. And veteran pilots often enjoy sharing their skills and experience with newly-minted pilots.

To get the best insurance rates for your flying club, provide agents with a roster of members and data on their personal information and their flying experience: names, birthdates, type license, ratings, total hours logged and in what make, model, and complexity. If the club operates a complex aircraft (such as RG or MEL), make sure the pilots who use it are up-to-date on their log requirements. Also note each pilot's data regarding accidents, incidents, submissions, losses, or DUIs. Your aviation insurance broker will want to know this – and probably penalize your club if they find out important facts after the policy has been issued. Even if you think the data is not fully relevant, include it as the insurance agent or broker will make the final decision as to what to include in the application to the insurance company. Your insurance broker is your partner in this transaction.

Choosing coverage

How much aviation insurance does your frugal flying club need? For the lowest policy price, keep the hull value at or below $100,000 per aircraft, at least for the first year of the policy. With a good record, you can increase the hull value if the actual value is higher.

For the best balance of coverage and costs, initially keep the liability limits at $1 million for each occurrence and $100,000 per passenger, recommends Bill Sneed. If appropriate, ask for quotes on higher liability limits. The difference in costs may be slight and offer greater peace of mind to flying club members.

On a related note, GAN recently covered "New benefits for flying clubs" as announced by the AOPA, offering free scheduling software and other tools and benefits to flying clubs. In addition to aircraft scheduling, it offers the club and members the capability to process credit card payments, create invoices, and other useful functions. Did I mention that it's FREE?!

Also, register your new frugal flying club with the AOPA Flying Club Network and review their Checklist for Starting a Flying Club. Take a look at http://www.aopa.org/Pilot-Resources/Flying-Clubs.

How Much Does Your Flying REALLY Cost?

Once a year – such as during bad flying weather – a frugal pilot should determine how much his or her flying habit REALLY costs. No, not the number that you tell your significant-other (nor the tax collector), the actual costs of owning or renting and flying an airplane. Calculating those costs annually is a good way to discover whether you're getting the most for each dollar you spend on flying.

Knowing the numbers doesn't mean that you're going to dramatically cut back – in fact, it may mean you spend more on some expenses. However, it does mean that you are focusing on value. Remember, a frugal pilot isn't cheap. She or he seeks value, safety, and fun.

The best place to start is to set up a spreadsheet, either on a computer or a tablet of paper. Electronic spreadsheets are easier as you can tell them to do the calculations for you automatically, and they are easier to update than paper. You can use Apple's Numbers, Windows' Excel, OpenOffice's (free) Calc, or any program that helps you set up, track, and update your flying budget.

Hopefully, you've kept all the receipts for money spent on flying. Once your spreadsheet is set up, future tracking of flying costs will be easier. Here's how to break down your Frugal Flying Budget:

Fixed costs are those expenses that go on whether you fly or not. If you own an aircraft, fixed costs include the cost of an annual inspection and repairs, insurance, ongoing maintenance (such as oil and filter), hangar or tie-down rent, association dues, taxes, and maybe interest on an aircraft loan. If you rent your aircraft, there may be no fixed costs – one of the many advantages of renting. If you're part of a flying club, your monthly membership dues may be the only fixed cost you have. If you're in a partnership, the fixed costs will be calculated, then split between the partners as outlined in the partnership agreement (equally, by hours flown, with deductions for service to the partnership, etc.)

Variable costs are the expenses that go up when you do. For aircraft owners, that means the cost of fuel and maybe oil if usage is significant. If you're renting "wet" (with fuel), the variable costs are included in your rental fee; otherwise, add your fuel purchases in. Partnerships typically pay full variable costs; the fuel you use is the fuel you buy.

The next step is to calculate total fixed and variable costs. This is where an electronic spreadsheet is really handy. For example, you list these costs in columns titled Per Year, Per Month, Per Hour, and Percent of Total. If you're comfortable with spreadsheets, you can include an editable cell that allows you to change the number of hours flown during a year (Hr/Year) to give you total and per-hour costs if you fly 25 hours a year versus 100 hours annually.

If you're really into frugal flying, you'll add a comparison of owning versus renting based on local rental rates. If oil-consumed is an issue, you can calculate a factor for replacement oil based on how many flight hours it takes to burn a quart of oil. You can calculate fuel costs based on current price and burr rate at 65% vs. 75% power. Get creative.

There is one other cost factor that can be significant in your calculations: **Replacement costs**. It's typically a variable cost based on how many hours are flown. The ownership question is: how are you going to pay for something not covered by insurance, such as a lost engine or a major repair? It's a legitimate question that aircraft owners and partners (not renters, of course) answer in various ways. Some owners say: I'll deal with it when it happens. Others say: Let's set aside some money for each flight hour to pay for potentially high repair costs. Partnerships often do this. But no one really knows when a major expense will come along, so some owners and partnerships set up a Reserves fund and pay into it for every hour flown. It could be a percentage of variable costs (such as 25%) or it could be calculated based on the difference between tach/Hobbs time and the estimated Time Between Overhaul (TBO) on the costliest items: engine and propeller. Still others simply add an estimated number to their Variable Costs, such as $10-an-hour, to help cover major repairs. The decision of how to handle major, often unforeseen, expenses is a big one for all aircraft owners – frugal or otherwise.

Once your Frugal Flying Budget is set up and populated, you can easily perform what-ifs: What would costs be if I flew twice as many hours a year, if I took on a partner, if I rented instead of owned, if fuel prices (variable costs) went down, if I upgraded avionics (fixed costs), if I paid off a loan or found lower-cost insurance? These and other scenarios can help you get greater value from each dollar you spend as a frugal pilot.

BONUS:
How to Become a Frugal Pilot

This publication assumes that you already are a licensed pilot who wants to fly on a budget. But what if you're not yet a pilot? What do you need to be a licensed pilot? Let me summarize the process.

To fly an airplane in the United States (Canada and other countries have similar processes), you must be at least 17 years old and you need to pass two tests:

- Knowledge Test – Written test requiring a passing grade of 70 percent or more.

- Practical Test – An oral examination and a flight test performed by a certified flight examiner.

For a Private Pilot Certificate, you also will need at least 40 hours of logged flight experience including flight instruction performed by a certified flight instructor and solo flight experience. Sixty to 70 hours is more typical. Younger students seem to require less training than older students.

For a Sport Pilot Certificate, you will need at least 20 hours of logged flight experience including flight instruction performed by a sport flight instructor and solo flight experience. The typical Sport Pilot requires 35-40 hours of experience to earn a certificate.

What's the difference between a Private Pilot and a Sport Pilot?

A Private Pilot can fly many general aviation aircraft under visual flight rules (VFR) day or night and, with additional training and testing, instrument flight rules (IFR). A Private Pilot is required to pass a Third Class Medical examination.

A Sport Pilot can fly two-seat light-sport aircraft under VFR rules during daylight hours only. A Sport Pilot only needs a driver's license to comply with medical requirements.

The good news is that to fly yourself (no passengers) you only need a Student Pilot Certificate which you can get by passing a Knowledge Test, satisfying your instructor that you can perform basic flight operations including takeoffs and landings, and get your Third Class Medical, if required. Most people earn their Student Pilot Certificate in less than 20 hours of flight instruction.

Actually, there is more to getting a pilot license than is summarized here. Much more. But this will help you start. Begin with an introductory flight from a nearby flight school (call your local airport), get enrolled in a ground school (theories and requirements of flying), find a certified instructor and rental aircraft, and get started. Additional guidance is available online at http://flighttraining.aopa.org/learntofly/.

Then review the many practical articles in this document to help you learn to fly on a budget as a Frugal Pilot.

See you in the pattern!

THE FRUGAL PILOT
How to Fly on a Budget

by Dan Ramsey

is published by Mulligan Press

About the Author:

Dan Ramsey is the best-selling author of dozens of books for consumers on aviation, business, and household topics (DanRamseyBooks.com). He also is Publisher at Mulligan Press (MulliganPress.com). In his spare time, Dan is Airport Manager at a community airport in northern California to help fund his flying habit. Until recently, Dan flew a 1959 Cessna 150, nicknamed "Goofy". He now rents his wings as a Frugal Pilot. For more information on flying on a budget, visit FrugalPilot.com.

8584013R00066

Printed in Germany
by Amazon Distribution
GmbH, Leipzig